demystifying DYSLEXIA

Raising Awareness and Developing Support for Dyslexic Young People and Adults

Contents

Introduction — 3

I What is Dyslexia?

An overview	5
Definitions	6
"Thick, lazy, careless or dyslexic?" - Labelling or liberation?	10
Dyslexia: a pattern of difficulties	13
Implications for learning	21
The experience of dyslexia	25
Sub-types of dyslexia	33
Dyslexia and speakers of other languages	36

II The Dyslexic Learning Style — 39

III Theoretical Perspectives

Neuropsychological perspective	47
Cognitive perspective	58
Developmental perspective	65

IV How Can I Help?

Supporting dyslexic students in further and higher education	69
Guidelines for tutors and lecturers	75
Setting up a learning programme	80
Technological and learning aids	88
Employment, training and careers	91

V Resource and Activity Sheets

Dyslexia : a pattern of difficulties	(Resource Sheet 1)
Common features of dyslexia	(Resource Sheet 2)
Am I dyslexic? Self-check	(Resource Sheet 3)
Identifying difficulties	(Resource Sheet 4)
Dyslexic learning style : implications for learning	(Resource Sheet 5)
Dyslexic learning style : strengths and weaknesses	(Resource Sheet 6)
Areas of difficulty for dyslexic students	(Resource Sheet 7)
Help in the classroom	(Resource Sheet 8)
How can I help? Case studies	(Resource Sheet 9)
How can I help? Supporting students	(Resource Sheet 10)
How can I help? Student writing	(Resource Sheet 11)
Routes to training and education	(Resource Sheet 12)
How can I help? Employment, training and careers : case studies	(Resource Sheet 13)
Twenty Questions	(Resource Sheet 14)

Glossary   i

References   iv

Recommended Reading and Resources   vii

Introduction

There are few disabilities that excite such controversy or evoke such powerful reactions as dyslexia. Indeed, its very existence is still questioned by some in spite of 100 years of research into its nature and possible causes.

Like a master of disguise and magic, dyslexia masquerades as inattention, carelessness or stupidity and teases by seeming to appear and disappear at will. It is invisible, yet seems to be responsible for such a range of things: poor spelling, messy handwriting, misunderstood instructions and missed appointments. No wonder it is greeted with suspicion!

Yet when we get to know it, its features begin to reveal themselves; we can see through the disguises and observe how it operates.

Young people and adults with dyslexia can tell us much about it: how it affects communication, writing, reading, remembering, organisation, direction, time - and other people. Research also can help us understand the cognitive, neurological and developmental aspects and their possible interrelationships. And observation of dyslexic people in learning situations can illuminate the dyslexic learning and thinking style.

Discovering and uncovering dyslexia can also give us great insight into learning itself - how we learn language, store and retrieve information, order and organise ideas.

This book is inspired by tutors of dyslexic students and their struggle to make sense of the puzzling features of dyslexic learners in attempting to meet their learning needs. It is aimed at all those who teach, advise and support dyslexic young people and adults. We have tried to take some of dyslexia's mystery away in order to increase consciousness of the role of cognitive and perceptual strengths and weaknesses in the learning process and in success in education and training. We approach dyslexia from a wide range of perspectives: how it is defined, its characteristics, its basis in theory and research, its emotional and practical effects and its implications for learning. We also offer suggestions for providing support for dyslexic students within further and higher education.

We include a number of photocopiable resource and activity sheets to be used in conjunction with the text for staff development and to stimulate discussion.

Introduction

Working with dyslexic people over many years has shown us not only the disability but the abilities they have, often untapped and distressingly lost in experiences of failure, frustration and confusion. We believe that understanding dyslexia is the key to improving learning and success for dyslexic people. We hope this book will be a resource for developing this understanding and thus help to alleviate some of the misery and frustration and unlock the potential of dyslexic young people and adults.

1 What is Dyslexia?

An overview

The term 'dyslexia' is derived from the Greek: 'dys' meaning hard or difficult and 'lexia' from the word 'lexikos' which means pertaining to words; so dyslexia means a difficulty with words - either *seen, heard, spoken* or *felt* as in writing. It is therefore appropriate to call it a "veritable syndrome of language-impairments" (Critchley, 1970). It usually affects an individual's ability to read quickly and efficiently and nearly always results in poor or 'bizarre' spelling, problems with written expression and difficulties with order and organisation.

Historically, dyslexia was originally a medical term referring primarily to a disorder in reading and spelling due to some form of neurological dysfunction. The concept of dyslexia has been known for at least a hundred years, first identified as 'word blindness' where there was no identifiable neurological damage or other explanation for the inability to learn to read. Original neurological research was conducted by doctors to account for spoken and written language deficits in patients who had suffered strokes. The damage was found to have occurred in the left hemisphere of the brain and has led to the identification of the areas which control language. These areas have recently been confirmed through the use of current technology.

There is no clear agreement about the causes of dyslexia but there are many useful perspectives for understanding dyslexia: educational, cognitive, neurological and developmental. There are also social and emotional consequences which contribute to the problems and experience of the dyslexic person.

Dyslexia can be most usefully seen as a difficulty with automatic language processing affecting people in reading, spelling and writing and a difference in cognitive style which affects learning, organisation and memory. This means that dyslexic learners need to employ different and often more personally meaningful strategies in order to learn language based skills.

Such students cause concern because they fail to acquire written language skills through ordinary learning and teaching methods and often fail to progress or to succeed in examinations; indeed they frequently drop out of education altogether. In educational and work situations they often receive feedback which draws attention to their poor literacy skills and they may be discouraged from taking courses or jobs until they improve these. Consequently, they may be denied opportunities to develop their strengths, so their talents and abilities are lost to them and to us.

Estimates of the incidence of dyslexia range from 4% to 10% of the population, depending on how narrowly these difficulties are defined. In further education especially, where there are likely to be many students who failed at school or did poorly in academic areas, the proportion of dyslexic people is likely to be higher, particularly on practically based courses and among adult returners. Identification and support of these students is an important part of addressing underachievement in education, training and employment.

Definitions

Definitions are often useful because they tend to give a concise summary from which to proceed to further study. However, as you read this section, you will find no such definitive summary, but a variety of definitions, some of which may appear to be contradictory.

The range of definitions reflect the historical development of research on dyslexia and seek to show the scope of interest and differing attitudes towards those who have difficulties with reading or writing. It should be stressed that these definitions do not necessarily negate each other; the fact that one emphasises difficulties with reading, another organisational difficulties, while another focuses on language processing difficulties aptly demonstrates how complex and wide-ranging the nature of dyslexia is.

It is little wonder that the lay public (and some educationalists) are often sceptical about the existence of such a condition, given the genuine confusion as to what it is. Although more people now recognise that dyslexia exists, giving a precise definition is still difficult. Perhaps we should accept that a wide perspective is necessary to grasp the developing picture of the processing of language based tasks and why some people have difficulties with words.

Historical perspective

Difficulties with reading were once attributed to the term *'word blindness'*. This term became used in studies of children with reading difficulties, notably by Pringle Morgan (1896), who published an account of Percy, a boy of 14, whose "... great difficulty has been - and is now - his inability to learn to read".

The concept of 'word blindness' became more common due to the writing of James Hinshelwood, a Glasgow eye surgeon. His account of the term is as follows:

> *"By the term congenital word blindness, we mean a congenital defect occurring in children with otherwise normal and undamaged brains characterised by a difficulty in learning to read ... and where the attempts to reach the child by the ordinary methods have completely failed".*
> (Hinshelwood, 1917).

Samuel Orton, (1925) an American neurologist, regarded the term 'strephosymbolia' (a twisting of symbols) as more relevant than 'word blindness', and felt that the difficulty lay mainly with ineffective visual processing. He was the first to notice a correlation between reading difficulties and patterns of 'handedness' and 'eyedness'.

The terms 'word blindness' and 'strephosymbolia' are no longer commonly used for the syndrome of dyslexia, but the work of Morgan, Hinshelwood and Orton did much to make society realise that under-achievement in literacy was not necessarily due to lack of intelligence or effort.

Recognition in the twentieth century

World wide, dyslexia was beginning to get some recognition and the term 'specific developmental dyslexia' was defined as:

> "a disorder manifested by difficulty in learning to read, despite conventional instruction, adequate intelligence and socio-cultural opportunity. It is dependent upon fundamental cognitive disabilities which are frequently constitutional in origin."
> (World Federation of Neurology, 1968)

In Britain, dyslexia was largely ignored by the official establishment until the 1970s. In fact, there was much scepticism about the existence of such a condition as can be noted from the dismissive summary made by the DES in 1972: "The term 'dyslexia' is not susceptible to precise operational definition and serves little useful purpose". The report concluded:

> "We are highly sceptical of the view that a syndrome of 'developmental dyslexia' with a specific underlying cause and specific symptoms has been identified ....We think it would be better to adopt more usefully descriptive term, 'specific reading difficulties' to describe the problems of the small group of children whose reading (and perhaps writing, spelling and number).... [are] below the standards which their abilities in other spheres would lead one to expect"....
> (Tizard Report, Children with Specific Reading Difficulties, 1972).

The Warnock Report published in 1978, recommended that the term 'special educational needs' be used, and that dyslexia came under this broad category. This was the first time that dyslexia was accepted as needing additional support. However, there was still much suspicion concerning the use of the term '*dyslexia*', as it carried "theoretical baggage" and the phrase '*specific learning difficulties*' was encouraged.

Specific learning difficulties

In America, the debate was more developed. The definition below indicates the thoughtfulness given to defining the wide range of difficulties which may be included under the heading of specific learning difficulties:

What is Dyslexia?

> "Those children who have a disorder in one or more of the basic psychological processes involved in understanding or in using language, spoken or written, which disorder may manifest itself in imperfect ability to listen, think, speak, read, write, spell or do mathematical calculation. Such disorders include such conditions as perceptual handicaps, brain injury, minimal brain dysfunction, dyslexia and developmental aphasia. Such a term does not include children who have learning problems which are primarily the result of visual, hearing or motor handicaps, of mental retardation, or of environmental disadvantage."
> (United States Office of Education, 1970)

The term dyslexia is often used interchangeably with the phrase 'specific learning difficulties' or in the USA 'learning disabilities'. Specific learning difficulties may be perceived as a spectrum within which dyslexia can be identified if a number of specific indicators are present.

'Discrepancy' model

Research into the syndrome of dyslexia was occurring in Britain and definitions were being developed, notably by Critchley. These definitions rested upon the assumption that there had to be a discrepancy between the academic achievement and intelligence of the child. Thus Critchley put forward the concept of developmental dyslexia as:

> "a severe difficulty with the written form of language independent of intellectual, cultural and emotional causation. It is characterised by the individual's reading, writing and spelling attainments being well below the level expected based on intelligence and chronological age. The difficulty is a cognitive one, affecting those language skills associated with the written form, particularly visual to verbal coding, short-term memory, order perception and sequencing."
> (Critchley, 1970)

This definition was elaborated later:

> "Developmental dyslexia is a learning disability which initially shows itself by difficulty in learning to read and later by erratic spelling and lack of facility in manipulating the written as opposed to the spoken word."
> (Critchley and Critchley, 1978)

Dyslexia as "spelling/reading retardation"?

It is perhaps definitions which concentrate on "socio-economic opportunity" which present dyslexia as a middle-class problem. Researchers such as Rutter criticised and questioned the exclusivity of the definition from the World Federation of Neurology and the concept of "conventional instruction, adequate intelligence and socio-cultural opportunity". His conclusions stated:

"....the term 'dyslexia'... does not refer to any well-defined group of disorders. Rather it constitutes a hypothesis regarding the supposed existence of a nuclear group or groups of disorders of reading and/or spelling caused by constitutional factors genetic in origin. Or alternatively, it refers to a more heterogeneous group of reading disabilities characterised by the fact that reading/spelling attainment is far below that expected on the basis of the child's age or IQ. If the latter usage is employed, it is probably preferable to use the terms specific reading retardation, or specific spelling retardation which involve no theoretical assumptions."
(Rutter, 1977)

Rutter's studies were very influential in the 1970s and did much to influence educational opinion. However, we now realise that to regard dyslexia as merely a difficulty with reading and spelling is misleading, as most dyslexic people identify additional recognisable problems.

A difficulty with processing language

From the wide-ranging definitions quoted, it can be said that dyslexia is a generic term that has come to refer to an extraordinary difficulty experienced by otherwise normal children and adults in processing language which is apparently a result of constitutional deficiencies. There is still a notion that dyslexia manifests itself purely in reading and writing but as some of the definitions show, the difficulties experienced by dyslexic people affect other areas of cognition. Therefore, researchers in this country and abroad have begun to further examine dyslexia as a subtle language deficiency.

It may be more useful to examine dyslexia from a perspective of *inefficient processing of language*. Dr Harry Chasty (Director of the Dyslexia Institute) defines dyslexia as:

"......... an organising difficulty, usually congenital, occasionally acquired, which affects physical skill development in laterality, information processing in short term memory and perception and so causes significant interference in the development of language in the individual...."
(Chasty, 1981)

More recent definitions have focused on dyslexia as a problem with language processing. Vellutino for example, defines dyslexia as having:

" its roots in a dysfunction during storage and retrieval of linguistic information; phonological-coding deficits (inability to represent and access the sound of a word); deficient phonemic segmentation (inability to break words into component sounds); poor vocabulary development and trouble discriminating grammatical and syntactic differences among words and sentences. Far from being a visual problem, dyslexia appears to be the consequence of limited facility in using language to code other types of information."
(Vellutino, 1987)

What is Dyslexia?

"Dyslexia to me is when your brain is going at 150 mph - but it doesn't come down on paper"
(Elaine, student at Lambeth College)

Dyslexia - an opportunity to excel

We have tried to show that the syndrome of dyslexia is a subtle and complex syndrome, not easily defined. This last definition, however, provides not only a comprehensive overview of the difficulties but offers a more positive way to view dyslexia:

"Dyslexia is a neurological difference of dysfunction in persons of any IQ level, from below average to gifted. It is a neurological status which may cause academic difficulties and impede the ability to organise, plan and schedule effectively. As a status, it is permanent and irreversible. Many dyslexics have in common a history of frustration and failure, especially in school. The difficulties however, are surmountable. Dyslexics also have uncommon gifts, skills and talents in many fields; the creative arts, architecture, engineering, construction, mathematics, physics, electronics, computer sciences, law, medicine, banking and finance, sports, entertainment and others. In the best circumstances, dyslexia is an opportunity to excel."
(Tri Services National Institute of Training and Research in Dyslexia, United States of America)

"Thick, lazy, careless or dyslexic?" Labelling or liberation?

There are some in educational circles who condemn the use of the term 'dyslexia' because it "labels" people. In fact, many dyslexic young people and adults failed in school precisely because they were labelled as 'lazy', 'careless' and even 'thick' or stupid' and their dyslexia was not identified. Some have been classified as 'educationally backward' and placed in remedial classes or even special schools unsuited to their needs. Others have had secondary emotional and behaviour problems addressed without identifying the primary dyslexic difficulties. One student, for example, was sent to four or five psychologists and therapists for her reading difficulties, all of whom worked on building her confidence and none of whom identified the fact that print was unstable when she looked at it.

Many dyslexic young people and adults meet the same lack of understanding when they return to education and receive 'more of the same' as they did in school. It is therefore extremely important that the real nature of their difficulties is identified and that their learning needs are met in an appropriate, specific and immediate way to enable success rather than perpetuating failure.

What is Dyslexia?

Do you recognise any of these comments?

Can't you even copy from the board?

This writing is a mess! You are still being careless

You aren't making any effort!

How many times have I told you? Now listen this time!

PROOF READ YOUR WORK!

Lazy spelling!

This essay is totally garbled!

TRY HARDER NEXT TIME!

Try to pay attention this time!

Please answer the question!

Could there be another explanation?

When young people and adults have their difficulties with language processing explained to them and legitimised, they frequently experience a sense of liberation which can often empower them to progress in education, training and employment.

"I thought I was the only one who had this kind of problem - it was such a relief to have a name for it!"

The importance of diagnosis

The diagnostic process is in fact one of 'de-labelling' and the diagnosis of dyslexia enables a shift in self-perception and an opportunity to start to discover strengths as well as weaknesses. The most common experience is relief: "It's not my fault - it's not me being stupid".

"I always thought there was something wrong, but I couldn't put my finger on it"

What is Dyslexia?

"They said I was lazy and wasn't trying hard enough, but I knew I was trying hard enough!"

"When I found out I was dyslexic, I went home and took out a recipe book and baked a cake! - That was because I felt better about myself as a person"

"I thought maybe I had multiple sclerosis like my aunt because I was always dropping things"

Many dyslexic people have been bowed down by self-doubt, confused about their abilities or frustrated by repeated failure. They often have a poor self-image which may show itself in very diffident or aggressive behaviour. Once they begin to understand why they have had difficulties in the past and to separate out the difficulties from their intelligence and abilities, their whole posture, body language and attitude may alter along with their feelings about themselves.

After the diagnosis

"I knew I wasn't stupid, but I was always being treated as stupid"

"It's great that I've got something in common with Einstein"

"It was a relief to find that there was a name to it!"

The feeling of relief is often quickly followed by anger at "all the wasted years" of having been misdiagnosed as a 'slow learner' or simply ignored within the educational system. Many dyslexic people feel that had suitable strategies been adopted sooner, they would have been spared years of misery and self-doubt. They often need counselling to help them express and sort out their feelings. But being diagnosed can also be the beginning of a more positive belief in their capacity to learn and to achieve.

Problems with terminology

Problems with terminology abound because dyslexia is not a well-defined entity but is a syndrome of language processing difficulties. Dyslexic adults and young people may have various patterns of difficulties which impair their academic progress in varying degrees and which extend beyond problems with reading and writing. Each person may display a different manifestation of the syndrome and experience difficulties with different aspects of study or employment. The term 'dyslexia' does not embody a uniform condition. Consequently, the term 'specific learning difficulties' is preferred by many educationalists and educational psychologists because it refers to a spectrum of difficulties, whereas 'dyslexia' is sometimes defined rather more narrowly.

The main problem with the term 'specific learning difficulties' is that it is a term generally *only* used by educational psychologists and teachers of special needs; others may find it meaningless or confuse it with general or moderate learning difficulties, which leads to dyslexic people being assumed to be of low intelligence or ability.

However, the term 'specific learning difficulties' can be a useful reminder that dyslexic people pursuing a course of study or training will need a *specifically designed programme of support* to suit their particular perceptual and motor strengths and weaknesses and cognitive style.

Which term do dyslexic people prefer?

Ask them. In our experience, students prefer to be identified as dyslexic. The term 'dyslexia' does not have the pejorative connotation which 'learning difficulties' has.

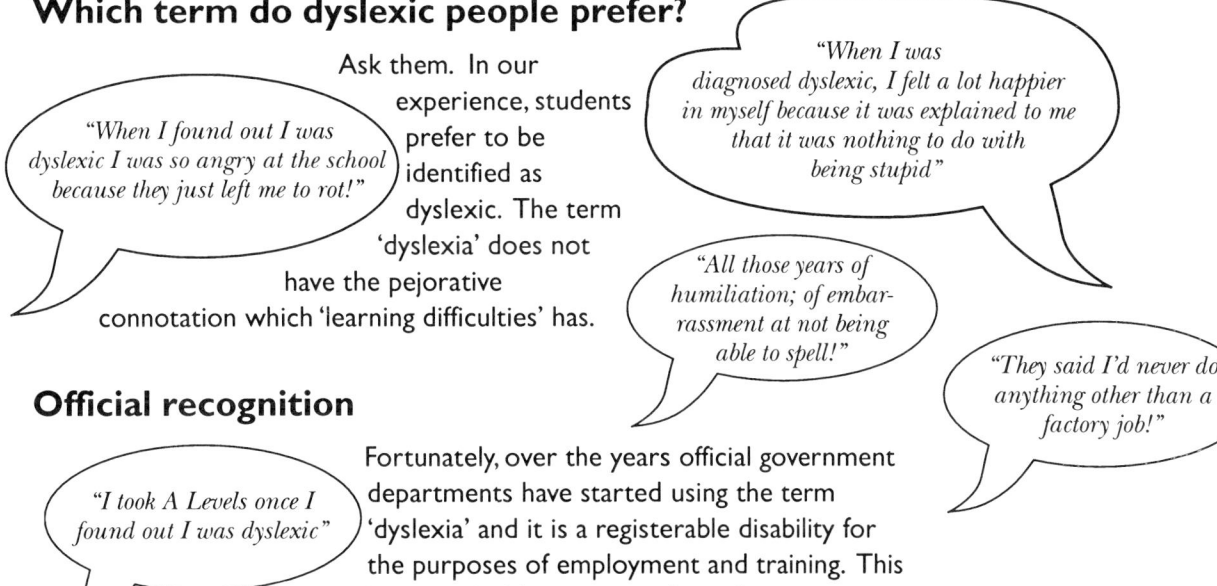

"When I found out I was dyslexic I was so angry at the school because they just left me to rot!"

"When I was diagnosed dyslexic, I felt a lot happier in myself because it was explained to me that it was nothing to do with being stupid"

"All those years of humiliation; of embarrassment at not being able to spell!"

"They said I'd never do anything other than a factory job!"

Official recognition

"I took A Levels once I found out I was dyslexic"

Fortunately, over the years official government departments have started using the term 'dyslexia' and it is a registerable disability for the purposes of employment and training. This has been invaluable in terms of equal access not only to further and higher education, but also to certification, support and equipment to help in employment.

Examination Boards make suitable provision for students who have been diagnosed as being dyslexic or having specific learning difficulties.

The Department for Education and Employment recognises the condition and students showing evidence of dyslexia may be eligible for a disability grant when entering higher education. Dyslexia is one of the learning disabilities eligible for funding for additional support under the funding arrangements of the Further Education Funding Council.

Dyslexia: a pattern of difficulties

Before one attempts to explain what dyslexia is, it may be useful to state what it is *not*:

It is not:

- a result of low intelligence
- related to class or ethnic origin
- a result of poor eyesight or hearing
- a result of an emotional problem
- an impediment to a possible academic career
- a middle class excuse for poor academic attainment
- a mental handicap

- an excuse to get preferential treatment in education or employment
- only a difficulty with reading or spelling

Dyslexia is (among other things):

A syndrome of difficulties which shows itself predominantly in written language. This term describes a developmental pattern of learning which does not favour an easy acquisition of fluency in language, especially with the written word. It is not a defect, but an individual difference in cognitive style, often associated with problems in sequencing, organising, time and direction.

Not all dyslexic people will experience difficulties in all the areas outlined below. Most may manifest only some of these signs, so it is important to look for *a **pattern*** of difficulties.

Indicators of dyslexia may include:

- **A marked discrepancy between ability and the standard of work** being produced. This is perhaps the clearest 'warning bell' that a student may have difficulties with processing written language.

    "I wrote it six times and then I tore it up because it was still rubbish"

    "I looked at the exam and knew most of the answers, but I couldn't write them down so I just left"

    "I turned down the promotion because I would have to write reports"

- **A discrepancy between evident intelligence and ability to learn** what appear to be simple language based skills. Dyslexic people are often frustrated or embarrassed by their poor literacy and may drop out of courses which intellectually they are capable of following or may refuse jobs which they could do well.

    "I know what I want to say but I can't find the right word"

- **A problem with word retrieval.** Individuals often know the word they want to use but "can't get it out".

    "I have to use a Thesaurus all the time. I look up a similar word I know, to get the exact word I need"

- **A problem with processing language quickly.** Individuals may be slow at taking in verbal information, and may lose track of what is being said.

    "I have to try so hard to keep up with what the lecturer is saying that my mind switches off"

    "I have problems in groups. By the time I take in what has been said, everyone else is already three steps ahead."

- **A persistent or severe problem with spelling, even with 'easy' or common words.**
The types of mistakes made will vary with the type of processing difficulty the person has. For instance:

What is Dyslexia?

Auditory processing difficulties.

People with these processing difficulties cannot match sounds to words or letters. They may have problems discriminating or 'holding' sounds. Writers with auditory processing difficulties often omit or confuse sounds within words or whole syllables.

"Fa-ther? Fa-th-er? What 'th' sound? Can't I just spell it 'fat-her'?"

Those with severe dyslexia sometimes find it difficult to know how to even begin writing a word.

> *[handwritten sample]*
>
> Young fledglings squabbled amongst themselves for the night ghost's praise. There she slept surrounded by a cocoon of living soft feathers.

Visual processing difficulties.

Individuals with these difficulties may have perfectly good sight but have difficulty in recognising when a word looks right or remembering the visual image of a word. They may have directional problems and so confuse similar looking ones like **b** and **d**, **p** and **q**, **m** and **w**.

"Through? Though? They look the same to me!"

"I have no image of the word 'other' - I do know how to spell it but I have lots of different things to remind me of how to spell it because I have no picture of what it looks like"

They are likely to spell phonetically and find particular difficulty with irregular spellings or ones where the sound doesn't give a clear indication of how the word looks. They have difficulties with homonyms and often mis-sequence letters.

witch from did you sing?
(which form did you sign?)

> *[handwritten sample]*
>
> Some people again were not too sure but at the end of it all everybody was wet to their waist

- **A difficulty with reading and comprehension.**

    Even advanced readers may have to re-read a text several times in order to gain comprehension. Again, the kinds of problems experienced by dyslexic people vary according to the severity and type of the processing difficulty.

What is Dyslexia?

Difficulties with auditory processing.

Readers with these difficulties find it difficult to decode new words as they are unable to use a phonic attack. As they cannot 'sound out' the unknown word, they rely on sight vocabulary and context to work out words they do not know. They therefore read for meaning and their comprehension can be very good. However, they have great difficulty with unfamiliar words or words out of context, as in multiple choice tests. If there are not enough words in a text which they recognise or clues from the context, their reading may be very inexact.

> "If I'm going to read the children a story, I practice beforehand to make sure I can pronounce all the words"

> "When its a story I'm OK, but when its a lot of names and new words I'm lost"

Difficulties with visual processing.

Readers with these difficulties find they often cannot recognise even familiar words. Consequently, when reading, they often have to work out the words from the sounds. This means that all their attention is going into decoding words, so they lose comprehension. They may also have difficulties with 'tracking' print and so omit either words or whole lines in the text. Even advanced readers may have to re-read material several times to understand it and are likely to misread.

> "Sometimes I look at a word like 'the' and it's as if I've never seen it before"

Other difficulties with reading may include visual distractions from unstable print, print which 'jumps out' of the page, 'halos' around words, 'blurry' letters, 'swirling' movements on the page which makes focusing on the visual image of the word impossible. Reading under such conditions is not only difficult but may be physically painful and extremely tiring for the person.

> "I decided to take up playing the guitar until I realised that every time I looked at the notes they were in a different place"

Students' experiences when reading:

"I see the hole in the 'p' instead of the 'p' itself"

"The letters start floating above the page and that's when I go to sleep"

"Each word has a 'halo' round it"

"After a while, the words begin to fall off the page"

"Some of the letters jump over each other so I can't tell what they are"

What is Dyslexia?

Some examples of distortions which students may experience:

"Blur" effect

"Swirling" effect

"Halo" effect

(For a detailed description of the difficulties and the use of colour to alleviate them, see Helen Irlen, Reading by the Colours, 1991)

- **A problem with directionality.**
  Most dyslexic people continue to confuse left and right. This has implications for recognising letters, reading from left to right, handwriting ("which way does this letter go?") and letter reversal confusions. They sometimes transpose numbers or the time when reading a clock.

  10 to or 10 past?

  Bus No. 23 or 32?

  'bone' or 'done'?

  "The keep-fit instructor kept saying 'left - right, back, forward - I just gave up in the end"

  "I put my letters back to front most of the time, no matter how vigilant and careful I try to be"

- **A weakness of short-term memory.**
  Dyslexic people usually have problems with short term memory; that is, their 'working memory' gets overloaded with having to cope with linguistic based tasks. They are inefficient and slower at effectively

  "Sometimes I spell a word right and can't remember it a few minutes later"

What is Dyslexia?

storing information into the long-term memory and then retrieving it. However, once they finally get the information into their long term memory, they rarely forget it. Their problems retrieving information are not caused by stupidity but by difficulties with coding either the visual or phonological aspects of language, or both.

Difficulties with short term visual memory.

These may include: difficulties in retaining, recognising and reproducing symbols (especially that of the printed language), directional confusion of letters or numbers or of sequences within words. The difficulties lie with coding visual linguistic information and not in interpreting general visual data. In fact, such persons may have excellent visual-spatial skills.

Difficulties with short term auditory memory.

These may include problems segmenting sounds and retaining sound sequences.

These difficulties affect reading and spelling but may also prevent

What is Dyslexia?

> *"I'm hopeless at following instructions because by the time the teacher's got to the end I've forgotten the beginning"*

correct understanding of what is heard or cause the dyslexic person with auditory difficulties to forget or confuse much of what is heard.

> *"I make mistakes in the equation because I copy the numbers wrong"*

> Someone moves in a graveyard Someone in A black hooded cloak the full moon Looms overhead glowing with unearthly. The figure pureses As if studing the grave stones.

- **A difficulty in motor integration.**

    This shows itself in poor handwriting (which may affect spelling as the student may not be able to control the pen), messy presentation of work or difficulty in forming the letters. Hand-eye and auditory-motor co-ordination may both be affected. When writing the person may unintentionally miss out or add letters or words. Handwriting is often very difficult to read or childishly formed and may mask the quality of ideas being expressed because the writer has to think about forming the letters. Sometimes a person's poor verbal articulation is a result of a problem with auditory motor co-ordination.

> *"As soon as I have to slow my thought processes to write, the words are like balloons and they all fly away"*

> *"I might start in the middle of a word or start with one word and halfway through write things that are not related to what I want to write - sometimes I write a different word altogether"*

> *"Sometimes I just can't get my mouth to say the right word - it just comes out wrong"*

- **A sequencing problem.**

    Dyslexic people often tend to think holistically or 'globally'; they remember the whole, rather than a series of what seems to be unconnected letters or steps. This means they may have problems following sequences,

A BRILLIANT ILLUMINATOR BUT ALAS, HE CANNOT CONTROL HIS SCROLLS.

demystifying DYSLEXIA

What is Dyslexia?

> Advantages of a Life Interest: it will secure the destiny of his capital when first selling trust property. It will be chargable for and subject to tax at 20%

"I've got lots of ideas but I can't think what to put down first"

instructions or procedures. It will also affect their writing. Their ideas, words and sentence structure get 'all jumbled up'. Despite this, the ideas are often contained within the piece of writing.

- **An organisational problem.**

"I had to give up my weaving class because I could never get all the sequences right"

Many dyslexic people appear to have difficulty with automatic organisation of two or more actions at one time. They therefore seem disorganised or clumsy. They may also have difficulties ordering information, organising their assignments or work and organising their time. They have problems categorising information or ideas.

"She told me to prioritise my work and I just couldn't do it"

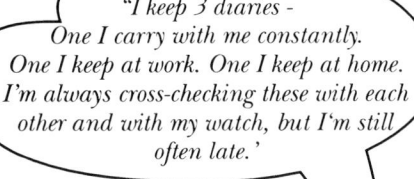

"I keep 3 diaries - One I carry with me constantly. One I keep at work. One I keep at home. I'm always cross-checking these with each other and with my watch, but I'm still often late.'

- *A difficulty with time*

Many dyslexic adults recall having difficulties in learning to tell the time when they were children. For some, these confusions still exist and they continue to transpose times. Some use a digital watch which overcomes the directional problems, though numbers my still be misread. However, many have a very vague concept of time. They know they have to be somewhere at a certain time, but unless they continually monitor the time and date, they do not sense how much has gone by or how long something will take.

"No matter how hard I try my folder is always a mess - I can never find my assignments or they're in the wrong place.'

Depending on the areas of difficulty in processing language, dyslexic people will experience a range of these difficulties, **but not necessarily all of them.**

Implications for learning

Spelling

Students who experience significant spelling difficulties even at an advanced level are likely always to have spelling difficulties. Each new word must be learned separately as generalisations are not automatically made. Spelling is usually also erratic - remembered one day and forgotten the next or even forgotten from one paragraph to the next.

While course work requirements may not specify perfection in spelling, the student with spelling difficulties is often very aware of the negative reactions of any reader to poor spelling. A student with severe spelling difficulties may need to look up as many as one out of every five to ten words in the dictionary. Some students have great difficulties in finding the word in the dictionary as they cannot even make a guess as to how the word is spelled. They may avoid using words they cannot spell with the result that their vocabulary and expression of ideas appears very limited.

Handwriting

Students with handwriting difficulties often have spelling difficulties as well. Specific tuition in handwriting is often needed, especially since many students have never been taught how to join up letters or were encouraged to print in earlier years because their handwriting was considered 'too messy'. Writing may be physically arduous. Some students have reported that their hand aches even after a short period of writing and that they cannot control the pen. In one instance a student reported that the pen 'flies across the room'. For others, forming letters takes so much concentration that their ideas get lost and their written expression suffers. Students with these difficulties usually benefit greatly from the use of a word processor and often their writing improves considerably.

Reading and comprehension

The most serious difficulty many dyslexic students encounter is the time it takes to read and understand a text or short excerpt. Reading becomes an arduous task. Students report that they get tired even during a short period of reading activity and may get headaches or even feel physically ill. Students may have to re-read material several times to understand it and are still likely to misread. Often, even advanced students experience problems taking in what they read even when they know all the words. Some with severe difficulties may need to use alternative sources of information such as tapes, as well as a reader in examinations.

Other students will be unable to work out unfamiliar words so a new course of study or new subject will create problems. Students may also find it difficult to recognise words out of context so multiple choice tests may cause difficulties.

Proof-reading

Dyslexic students (especially those with visual processing difficulties) have exceptional problems in identifying errors in their own writing. Because they are so unsure of how words are spelled, they cannot differentiate between correct and incorrect spellings. Reading difficulties make it hard for them to see their own errors in expression, sentence structure or grammar. These difficulties may be compounded by a poor appreciation of linguistic rules and structures.

Although a word-processor is an invaluable tool for dyslexic students, it sometimes gives a false sense of security. Often students think they have no spelling errors in a piece of work, as none were shown up by the spell-check. However, spell-checks cannot distinguish incorrectly used homonyms, real words or proper names.

Organisation, classification, categorisation

Dyslexic students continue to have exceptional problems in acquiring organisational skills necessary to progress in academic writing. They find it difficult to plan a piece of writing, to develop an argument and link ideas in a sequence. They may have all the ideas but be unable to order them. Sentence structure is often affected by students raising many ideas in one sentence, instead of organising these ideas into separate paragraphs. Students may also find it exceptionally difficult to determine what is relevant and irrelevant, as for them everything is connected to everything else.

This difficulty with organisation may manifest itself in untidy and messy folders to illogically constructed essays, even though in both folder and essay 'everything is there'. Consequently, the student cannot find the appropriate notes and has left the assignment somewhere else. Organising time and space may also be difficult; students may get lost easily and turn up at the wrong time or on the wrong date. A computer soft-ware programme such as 'Thinksheet' can be an enormous help as can a diary, colour coded folders and a personal organiser.

Vocabulary and written expression

Because of difficulties storing and retrieving language, dyslexic students take longer to acquire new terminology; they need more examples and practice to thoroughly acquire new words. This is true in spite of the mature verbal skills the student might possess. When writing, they also commonly experience great difficulty in 'finding' the words they want. As a result, some students use convoluted expressions and may write in a roundabout way, sometimes without realising it. Other students may be unable to express what they mean in a coherent grammatical form. Most dyslexic students find it particularly hard to grasp conventions of written language. For example, a student wrote "is construct" instead of "is constructed". When asked why, she explained that she had learned in English class that '-ed' was for the past tense and 'is' was present tense.

Note-taking

Note taking can be a particularly stressful task for the dyslexic student due to spelling difficulties, poor short term memory and sometimes difficulty taking in auditory information at a rapid pace. Dyslexic people are rarely automatic writers. As they have to think about each word they often miss out important points and lose track of the lecture. Often students are unable to read their own notes because they cannot listen and spell or write simultaneously. Dyslexic writing is often slower, as they may have problems both with processing language and with forming the letters.

Copying from boards or overhead transparencies also presents problems for students who may easily lose their place or be unable to 'hold' the words or letters in their memory long enough to write them down. The writing may be too small or unclear for the student to be able to form an impression of the word. Tutors often wipe the board before the student has a chance to write down what was written.

Memorisation difficulties

Students may have memorisation difficulties which result in taking longer to process information into their long term memory. They will often confuse names, dates and facts which have no meaningful association for them. Many dyslexic students experience difficulties with remembering spoken instructions. Revision for examinations takes longer and students need extra support in acquiring study skills and additional memorisation strategies based on their individual learning style.

Distractibility

Some dyslexic students find it difficult to concentrate and may be prone to distractibility. Their ideas are often 'all over the place' and it may take extra effort to focus on one task at a time or prioritise what is important. Others have 'nodded off' during the lesson from the relentless effort of having to concentrate to take in all the contributions to a discussion and all the information in a lecture. Outside noise or visual distractions may also affect their ability to take in what is being said.

Pronunciation difficulties

Some students may have continuing pronunciation problems with polysyllabic words even if those words are in their active vocabulary. They can never be certain that the words will "come out right". This may make them less confident when having to give presentations or participate in discussions.

Conclusions

Thus even advanced students may continue to have difficulties in:

- **reading assigned texts on time**
  even 'good' readers take longer to read texts

- **reading comprehension**
  if the student has visual processing difficulty

- **reading new words**
  if the student has an auditory processing difficulty

- **spelling**

- **handwriting**
  poorly executed, difficult to read, messy, immature

- **essay writing**
  with particular difficulties in organisation, written expression grammar and punctuation

- **proof-reading**

- **note-taking**

The experience of being dyslexic

"I have forgotten the word I intended to say, and my thought, unembodied, returns to the realm of shadows"
(Osip Mandelstam)

Introduction

The experience of being dyslexic has been eloquently and movingly described by many dyslexic people. The following selection from the writing of dyslexic young people and adults gives some of the flavour of being dyslexic and a sense of how it colours and shapes their lives.

Education

Recalling my feelings about school before finding out I was dyslexic is very hard because of no self confidence in me or my work and that made me very confused.

I found myself getting into trouble with the teachers, my parents and the police. The trouble with the teachers was for not keeping up with the class. They always put me at the back of the room or sent me out on odd jobs, but most of the time I fooled around in school and at home, so they just gave up on me. When I did work at school, my end of term reports were all quite good but all said the same thing: that I was lacking in commitment - but could you blame me?

The thing that hurt me so much about school was one of the teachers had the nerve to say to my face that I was so thick that I would amount to nothing! And I believed him.

* * *

During a period in the 6th form I had a break down when a teacher asked me to read aloud - a teacher who knew I had a reading problem. I tried to change her point of view with a chair. I left school: I was sixteen with no self esteem and a bad attitude.

* * *

It is hard to write about word blindness when you don't really know what it is, maybe it is easier to write about something you can see. Teacher Blindness or 'TB' for a start. This affects only one in so many teachers and could be due to many things: too many pupils, overworking or concentrating on the brighter members of the class.

'TB' happened to me gradually at junior school when nobody could see that I was the only person who was three books behind in reading, could not read out loud in class, could not spell and didn't know any times tables! The unfortunate remedy for this was a remedial reading class despite my being second in a general knowledge test.

My main problems at school were just that I could not do French because I could not do English. I could not do physics or chemistry because I could not understand chemical symbols, the periodic tables or equations and I misread a lot of examination instructions *but worst of all I did not know why.*

* * *

The school's action was to place me in remedial classes, which played a great part in my schooling. I became part of the "hardcore". By "hardcore", I mean we were put there in the first year and were still there in the fifth. The object of remedial class was to give extra help with reading and spelling. For some pupils the classes worked well and filled the criteria they were designed for. A few months in these classes, pupils caught up and went back to normal classes, but for the hardcore remedials this was not so.

The separation of these classes reinforced the stigma of backwardness. If only some thought was given to the needs of the members of these classes, how things could have been different! The question "Why are they not learning?" was never asked. Conventional methods of teaching had failed us, but they were still embodied in these classes: spelling tests, reading aloud, writing out spelling rules. Different people need different strategies to learn - it is just a matter of finding which one.

To have a disability that no one can see or understand is a lonely existence. Although able to compete with fellow pupils, socially and in other areas of school life, the thing that matters most - reading and writing - is not there. Just a void. The remedial classes physically separated you. The public humiliation you went through when your limitations were exposed in public also separated you. It pointed to a damning conclusion. That you were backward.

For the hardcore, when that conclusion has been reached, there are two roads. The first, blind fury and resentment that one cannot operate withi the classroom, so they step-out of the learning process. They mess around, causing as much havoc as possible. If they have been denied the means of learning, why should others learn?

The second path is the crushed individual. Far from challenging the world around them, they are personally restricted. Their self image has been repeatedly deflated and underrated through discrimination. They cannot take part in the activities, they have no confidence. So they do their best to become invisible, sitting in the classroom not drawing attention to themselves. Both paths stifle your most personal modes of expression, touching you to the core. Both these roads run in the same direction, under-rating potential and creating despair.

* * *

I hated spelling tests, my teacher never believed me when I said I had learnt my spelling for homework because I usually got 3/20. I was in tears when she made me write 'because' 200 times on the backboard in front of the class and much to the delight of some of them. I hated her and was frightened to death of her. It was humiliating to be forever failing in class.

I dreaded the exams, they made me feel ill. I felt different and didn't like most of the pupils in my class and they didn't like me. I wanted to do well and it appeared to me that most of the class could not care less what they achieved at school, but I was the thick one.

The achievement that helped me to keep my pride was Ballet Dancing. I went four times a week. I had a natural ability and the determination to do well at something. It was a different world from school. I was one of the Principal's star pupils and never achieved less than 95% in my exams. Thanks to her!

Looking back it didn't appear to matter to her that I danced to the left when the teacher told us to dance to the right. She asked my mother to let her have me for private lessons with her. She taught me through repetition and instilling self confidence.

Much to my mother's dismay, she always sent me into the ballet exams with a painful slap to my right leg and arm so I wouldn't forget which was my right side and my left side. And it took the conspiring look and encouraging signs in her eyes which did the rest. I passed every exam with honours. She was a hard task master but she was never sarcastic or impatient or humiliated me like the teachers at school did.

* * *

When I was at school I could understand words and I could read and write as long as the words were well spaced out. If I looked at a page with a lot of print I couldn't see the individual words and it gave me a headache. I could not even read my own handwriting. Despite this I knew I wasn't stupid.

I was very good at art and maths and enjoyed them very much. However, geography was my favourite subject. Nevertheless, to avoid writing on the topic I remember asking the teacher if she would let me make a model of a tea plantation. Also, during a reading session I would sit at the back of the classroom so that I could memorise the text off by heart. When I was asked to take notes, I would draw illustrations, then at home, I would ask my older sister to read aloud any work that I had to learn, so when the teacher the following day questioned me on the text, I was able to answer her, and it appeared that I had read the work.

* * *

I had always been told that I was stupid and I was inclined to believe this. I never excelled at school, I was a late reader and my writing and spelling have always been poor. Maths was non-existent. My school reports were often "must try harder"; as far as I was concerned, I had been trying as hard as I could.

I have always tried to avoid putting pen to paper and was very ashamed of my writing and lack of spelling properly. Somebody once told me that I only had to write a word on a piece of paper and the paper was spoilt, and I'm afraid that this stuck.

It was with numeracy that the real problems began for me. When I first started class, I was asked if I could count to a hundred. I thought what a silly question to ask, of course I could. But the more I thought about it, the more I realised I couldn't. It was all right until I reached fifty or sixty then it started going haywire. I would jump a number or lose myself completely. I could add up, my taking away was a bit shaky. I did not know my multiplication tables and that caused another problem. I could not understand why, when reciting them, that I would miss one out and jump up one. I did think once or twice if I was going mad. I couldn't make out what was happening. On long multiplication, no matter how many sums I did, I still made mistakes and I knew my tables this time. With long division, I occasionally would add the sum up instead of subtracting the sum. Algebra was the biggest problem and still is with the - and + signs.

* * *

Finding Out

How does one describe or begin to describe the many different feelings and emotions which hit you in the after shock of the earthquake diagnosis. Deep down I had always known something was wrong. I can remember my reading and writing skills had been a source of embarrassment in public and, when I was old enough to care, private torture.

Looking back it seems all too easy to remember the educational equivalents of public mutilation or tar and feathering, features of my school life. I remember the humiliation, and far from forgiving my tormentors today, I would not pass up the opportunity to get even - it still hurts that bad.

Positive diagnosis is a shock, asking around it seems to affect fellow dyslexics in a personal and profound way. For myself I remember a tremendous tidal wave of relief - overwhelming, drowning relief. I was not stupid, dumb, slow, lazy, hopeless, backward. I was dyslexic and I could do something about it, the question was what? The effect of being diagnosed, coupled with deeply held emotions, came the dubious prospect of shedding tears in public; in short, I felt like crying.

* * *

When I was diagnosed, the tutor began with asking me questions and to read a sheet of words which I was unable to do. She then asked me to write down what she read to me and if I would read it back to her - *I could not.* Next, she gave me back the sheet of paper with a lot of print on, inside a blue plastic folder and asked me if I could read it. I could see the words although it didn't make any difference. She then replaced it with a red one. I could not look at it, my eyes started to hurt, I got a headache and I felt sick so I pushed it away from me. The red folder was changed to a yellow one and almost straight away I could feel myself relaxing, plus I was able to read it. Then the yellow folder was changed to a green one and I was able to read it too. I was excited! It was amazing! *I could read it!*

* * *

I have much more confidence in myself and now know which mistakes are due to dyslexia. I have realised I have found ways around a lot of problems. I feel as if a ton weight has been lifted off my head.

* * *

On finding out that I was dyslexic I felt relieved because at last there was an explanation of why things kept on going wrong and why my spelling was so erratic, or why I had problems learning the times tables and why I had so many problems with my writing.

I also felt very angry that it hadn't been diagnosed at school and that it had taken so long for me to find out what the problem was. I felt cheated out of my education. I felt I wanted to talk to somebody about it to discuss it. I felt very much alone and isolated. I found a book about dyslexia and found it very helpful but I still felt the need to talk to my husband but he didn't believe in dyslexia and is still very sceptical about it.

I think that for the first time in my life somebody was saying that I was intelligent. It was just that it was hard to accept. For most of my life I have been told how stupid I was and now there was somebody saying that I was intelligent.

* * *

What it's like

The way dyslexia affects me in life is mainly confusion with communication with others.

* * *

My reading is very slow as the lines merge together and the words jump off the page at me. This makes my eyes sting especially after reading or using the word processor for longer than two hours. Thus reading is extremely difficult and time consuming.

My spelling is affected tremendously. I put my letters back to front most of the time, no matter how vigilant and careful I try to be. I make constant mistakes. My hand writing is often difficult to read; I find a rub-out pen essential.

* * *

What is Dyslexia?

Sometimes when I pick up a book I can read it and other times it looks like a foreign language. I feel as if there is a piece of jigsaw puzzle missing and if I could find it, everything would fall into place.

* * *

When I read, the writing goes into one black line. I also have a problem with some of my writing, I might start in the middle of a word or start with one word and half way through write things that are not related to what I am writing. I sometimes write a different word altogether. When I read I have a problem in breaking words up. Words I don't know I miss out hoping I can find out what it might mean as I read on.

If I can't grasp a problem or a word, I find that my mind will close the shutters. I try and try until my head hurts, then I say my brain has overworked.

* * *

Despite my condition I enjoy writing even on this clapped out old typewriter. The thing I find difficult is keeping my writing flowing, as I have to think about the spelling of the word (even though I'm not too worried about getting it perfect). It is still too interuptive. In my mind I will think three, four or five sentences out, which flow on into one. My mind is beginning to get this heavy, confused, fussy feeling. It feels like I'm doing something which my mind is telling me is no good for me. I can feel the energy draining out of me and my eyelids getting heavier and heavier. The eyelids, being the doors to this exercise, seem to refuse to take in any more data.

* * *

It is difficult to put into words what it is like being dyslexic. The difficulty lies not in describing how I am but in trying to imagine how other people are, to pick up a book and read as easily as most people walk. To read abstract facts from a text-book and remember them or to write something as simple as a cheque in a bank. This is a big one - to stand between two people, one behind the counter, one behind you and to have your cheque passed back to you with usually a curt reminder the you spell 'fifty', *fifty* not *fiffty*.

* * *

I could cry, maybe it's because I am not correcting the spelling before someone else sees it, my barrier is down and I need help. Where does this leave me, where can I start, will it get better?

I don't even know how to correct this page, it would take me a long time to look up each word in the dictionary, and then it doesn't help the grammar. It's not that I am afraid of learning, it's that I am afraid of not remembering what I learn. To me this is frustrating and makes me give up easily!

* * *

My ability to tell left from right improved enormously once I got married (no, it was not the result of contentment!) - it was because I always wear my wedding ring on my left hand. It's not the whole answer though; if I've really got my wires crossed I can get it wrong, even when I've checked carefully with the ring. But I get it right most of the time nowadays - and when you're used to directional chaos, that's good enough!

* * *

The exercise was to takes notes or write a review. I had not completed one sentence before tripping over so many difficult spellings that I wanted to give up.

Even the structure of this piece of writing was daunting enough. It took me at least three hours to achieve a half page review. If only I could write as I speak; normally it comes out in the wrong order. I know roughly what letters go into a word like 'speak' but as the pen moves along the line they fall in the wrong order.

This I find very, very frustrating. It seems everybody else has this skill but me. I know this is not true but somehow this does not help. You could say it doesn't matter, I got through the last 30 years since I left school, but this has stopped my growth, not only in writing but in my self-esteem. It's rather like having a skeleton in the cupboard waiting to fall into your life - it's your own personal secret. Only now, perhaps, because I have developed myself in other ways, can I be honest. But only to people I trust.

* * *

On my nursing course, learning was difficult.; I had to learn anatomy by relating this to my own self image which was the only way I could remember where the bones and organs were. I would have pictures and notices on the door to learn something as I went through the doors.

Note taking was really difficult; therefore after each lecture I borrowed my colleague's notes as I could not make head or tail of my own notes. I had to stay in day after day and night after night, learning my notes, re-writing them which would take hours. Even then, copying them I would make mistakes. When copying off the board, I would often leave chunks out or repeat the same paragraph.

Sometimes I spell a word right and a short while after I cannot remember it; it escapes me and I am left struggling to retrieve it. Even when writing it down I may not recognise if it is right or wrong, or when I write it in five different ways!

Motor co-ordination does not help as I do not get the feel of it when writing it down. Also my hand will write something other then what my brain is wanting. This is frustrating. I have great difficulty in getting words out. It is as though there is a brick wall that you can't climb over. Sometimes my brain will say it but there's no sound.

When I told a few people at work that I was dyslexic some were understanding while others were patronising. I have terrible trouble remembering names and sometimes I get the names of doctors mixed up.

It was a struggle to remain cheerful as I discovered more about the nature of my difficulties and realised how much hard work it was to get things sorted out. Being diagnosed dyslexic and struggling by no means solved the problems but did help me to move on and I am glad I persevered.

* * *

Life after school was no easier. Letters and forms for jobs had to be written, one word at a time and checked for mistakes. This takes hours. One employer actually shocked me because he did not believe that the person who was taking the phone messages was the same person who wrote the letter that got the job.

Leisure activities are always a great form of escape from this sort of problem, unless of course you play Trivial Pursuit games where you have to read out cards containing questions or electronic pub quiz games, where the person who is clever enough to read out the question first always answers it wrongly, before you have even read two words.

I decided to take up playing the guitar until I realised that every time I looked at the notes, they were in a different place. Maybe one day they will stand still.

Sub-types of dyslexia

When a person with spelling and writing difficulties comes for a diagnosis, there are often several indicators pointing to a syndrome of dyslexia. Although there is a continuum of difficulties, there are three main areas of language processing difficulties which can be identified. Someone may have difficulties in one, two or all three of these areas, but usually one or two difficulties predominate.

Visual processing difficulties

People with visual processing difficulties may find visual perception of print problematic. They may complain that letters do not 'hold still' or that the print is blurred or jumpy, so that they cannot easily distinguish the shape of letters or words. When processing written language their visual memory is very weak and they find it difficult to re-visualise such material. They may have difficulties with sequence, order and direction.

When reading, they may have great difficulties recognising even familiar words and thus they rely on phonological 'sounding out', often without too much difficulty. They are frequently disturbed by inconsistencies in print and often lose their place or miss lines within a text. They misread irregular words such as *colonel* or *seizure* and regularise words to fit a phonic schema already established: for example, *steek* for *steak*. Their reading style may be relatively fluent but with a tendency for a jerky or word by word delivery, often ignoring punctuation. As all the attention is used to decode the words rather than recognising them directly, comprehension is often very poor, or a passage has to be re-read several times.

Their spellings are usually good phonic alternatives, but may lack significant visual features, eg *ekoing* for *echoing*; *lisend* for *listened*; *nife* for *knife* or *noyzey*

What is Dyslexia?

for *noisy*. They often use the wrong homophone. Since they have poor visual recall, they cannot remember letter sequences or letter patterns, as in *lenght* for *length*. Copying from books or the blackboard can be a daunting experience.

Problems with maths may be common: they often misread or missequence numbers, confuse signs such as + and x and have difficulties with 'place' as in long division or decimals.

Auditory processing difficulties

People with auditory or phonological processing difficulties have particular difficulty with letter-sound correspondence. They may have a poor memory for sounds or have difficulty discriminating or sequencing them. Other difficulties may be with chunking units of sound and with expressive language skills. For instance, they may have difficulties retrieving names or 'finding' the word they want to use. There is often a correlation with problems with 'taking in' rapid speech, as in lectures or lengthy oral instructions.

When reading, they cannot fully utilise phonic strategies so cannot read unknown or unfamiliar words. They are forced to depend on the visual appearance of a word and lexical or meaning-based 'chunks' to build up a bank of words they can recognise on sight. When faced with a word they cannot recognise while reading, they will often substitute a word which fits the context. Their reading style may be very slow and hesitant as they often rely on contextual cues in order to work out words which will give meaning to their reading. Although the reading process is often stressful and slow for them, their reliance on context means that their comprehension is often excellent if there are enough words they know. However, if there are not enough clues in the context or they don't know enough words, comprehension may be vague.

> Recently my brother Michael bought a new video recorder. It's a very technical piece of equipment. It has so many knobs and buttons on it and they all have such fancy names. It took Michael two hours just to get some kind of order out of it, and even now two weeks later, it is still far from perfect, but given time I'm sure he will master it.

Spelling is often bizarre, showing little representation to the original spelling eg *cultester* for *collection*; *grousmum* for *gruesome*; *sliecnce* for *silence*; *cralle* for *trial*. In other cases, sounds or blends are missing, confused or missequenced as in *cate* for *craft*; *trouse* for *trousers*; *grode* for *glowed*; *volient* for *violent*; *sepate* for *separate*.

If there are problems in maths, they are usually to do with memorising difficulties and with the language of maths.

Motor processing difficulties

Motor processing or motor integration difficulties can usually be identified by looking at a student's handwriting and organisation of work. The handwriting is often messy, badly formed and sometimes illegible; the ideas contained in an essay are often disjointed and seem to 'rush out' without a coherent form or structure. For such students, writing never becomes automatic. They often have the experience of their "hand not doing what they want" and so produce work with much crossing out of words and letters omitted or repeated. Sometimes handwriting may look all right but eye-hand co-ordination may be poor, with letters oddly joined, 'fused' together or missing. Their written expression often improves greatly on a word processor, where the effort of forming letters is removed.

Difficulties controlling their writing may mean their hand gets tired when writing for even short periods; thus their handwriting commonly deteriorates in timed conditions. Spelling errors frequently include 'telescoping', as in *rember* for *remember*, whereby the person fails to keep track of multi-syllabic words due to poor eye-hand co-ordination and 'perseveration' or inability to stop repeating a motor pattern, as in *machinine* for *machine*.

Motor processing difficulties are often closely related to difficulties with visual processing, in which case reading difficulties may be manifested by difficulties in keeping track of the words or following the line of print. Letters, words and sometimes whole lines may be 'lost'.

Dyslexia and speakers of other languages

Identifying dyslexia in people for whom English is a second or even third or fourth language is obviously much more complex. Features of the first or other languages may account for difficulties discriminating certain sounds, spelling errors, lack of writing fluency and awkward expression or grammar. Where the first language has no written form or a very different script, acquiring handwriting skills may be a problem. Consequently, it is important not to assume that all such problems are the result of dyslexia.

However, it is equally important not to assume that all problems are to do with learning a new language. Many people acquire a second or third language without much difficulty. Those who speak two or more languages are frequently more sophisticated in understanding how languages work than monolingual speakers.

Too many young people and adults have their persistent failure to progress, even over several years, put down to being a second language speaker. There are some indicators which should alert teachers of those whose first language is not English to the possibility of dyslexia as a factor in lack of progress:

- an unexpectedly great discrepancy between their mastery of spoken English and their poor writing skills

- a striking difference in the types of spelling errors they produce from those of students with a similar language background

- erratic and inconsistent spelling - 'good' and 'bad' days, or words spelled many different ways on different occasions

- great difficulty in acquiring and applying the rules of grammar, that is generalising grammatical structures

- noticeable and unusual problems with some classroom activities, such as copying from the board, grammar and vocabulary drills and exercises, putting into sequence pictures, sentences or ideas

- uncommon difficulties in organising their work.

They may also be slower to pick up and retain oral language. Unpublished research by Lindsay Peer suggests that there are two profiles of difficulty for dyslexic bilingual speakers. The first type seems to be able to acquire the first language fairly well but the memory capacity breaks down when trying to learn the second language. This results in failure to learn the second language adequately, or learning it but at a cost of losing proficiency in the first language. The second type speaks both languages well enough to get along but memory overload interferes with development of full competence in either.

A careful approach to analysing errors and an appreciation of a student's learning style can help to identify difficulties which may be due to dyslexia rather than to second language features. It is also extremely valuable to have someone with the same first language to help identify a student's problems in that language. Although dyslexia may be expressed differently in different languages, people who are dyslexic will be so in their first and other languages as well as in English.

II - The Dyslexic Learning Style

"the problem of dyslexia is an individual difference in learning style"
(Michael Thomson, 1990)

Dyslexia can be seen as a differing cognitive style. Dyslexic persons have (as do other people) strengths and weaknesses in how they process and organise information within the brain. Understanding these strengths and weaknesses can help tutors, employers, employees and students find more effective approaches to organising learning and work.

> ### What do we mean by the term 'learning style'?
>
> A learning style is above all, a particular cognitive style, and:
>
> *"[one] that accounts for individual differences in a variety of cognitive, perceptual and personality variables."* (Vernon, 1973).
>
> Or represents:
>
> *"a person's typical modes of perceiving, remembering, thinking and problem solving."* (Messick 1976)
>
> It is therefore a broad term to describe factors which influence all aspects of an individual's learning and can be summarised as:
>
> *"... characteristic cognitive, affective and physiological behaviours that serve as relatively stable indicators of how learners perceive, interact with, and respond to the learning environment."* (NASSP, 1979 from Keefe, 1987)

A learning style can therefore be seen as the practical manifestation of a person's processing strengths operating in natural learning contexts. For example, a child with a highly developed spatial intelligence may show a preference for, and a superiority in, learning about new things through pictures, drawing activities, three dimensional building materials, videotapes and computer programs containing graphics (Dunn R, 1985; Armstrong, 1994). These natural talents, or 'intelligences' as Howard Gardner (1985) would call them, are likely to continue into adulthood.

Teaching methods in our society are largely focused on activities which rely on language and the consequent need to process a great deal of verbal information in one form or another. Such an approach favours students who have no difficulties with processing language efficiently or using a sequential approach to learning.

The Dyslexic Learning Style

SO WHAT I GOT THE KNIVES AND FORKS THE WRONG WAY ROUND? SO I PAINTED 'EM OUT.

Because dyslexic learners have inadequately developed language specialisations in the left hemisphere, they often rely more on right hemisphere functioning. Consequently, they develop a preferred learning style which reflects this processing bias, favouring a holistic and visual-spatial approach, rather than one which is sequential, temporal and language based.

Dyslexic people have some weakness in working memory, that is holding, storing, retrieving and manipulating linguistic information. As a result, they must make meaningful, often highly personal connections in order to learn and remember. The advantage of this is that they often have excellent long-term memories.

Not all dyslexic people will exhibit this cognitive style and not all will have strong visual-spatial skills. However, 'right brain' approaches to learning are usually more effective for two reasons: first, because the dyslexic learner is definitely disadvantaged in some aspects of left hemispheric linguistic processing and second, because right hemispheric approaches are powerful tools for learning generally as they emphasise emotion, humour and imagery.

Since the first research into hemispheric differences, attempts have been made to identify and classify the functions of the two halves of the brain. The following is a typical attempt to define the specialisations of the two hemispheres.

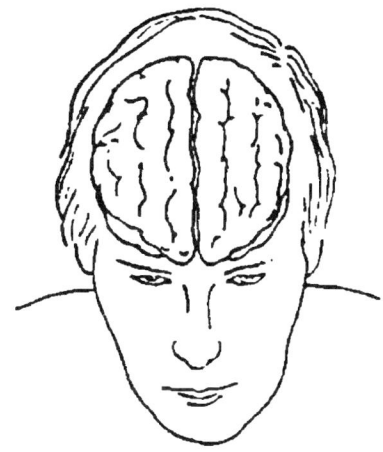

Hemispherical specialisations of the brain

LEFT BRAIN	RIGHT BRAIN
Linear progression	**Global approach**
Sequential - A to B to C	**Simultaneous -** complex inter-relationships
Temporal - one at a time	**Spatial -** all at once
Looks at the **particular**	Looks to the **whole**
Looks for **cause and effect**	Looks for **inter-relationships**
Uses language to name, describe, define	**Uses pictures**, shapes and colour
Analytical - breaks things down	**Constructional**, pattern-seeking
Deductive - draws conclusions through a logical progression from the general to the particular	**Inductive -** draws general conclusions from an intuitive basis and a variety of sources
Keeps to the **facts**	Makes several redundant **elaborations** in an idiosyncratic manner
Knows **'how'**	Discovers **'what'**
Thinks in signs - remembers complex motor sequences	**Thinks in design -** remembers complex images

The Dyslexic Learning Style

Common features of the dyslexic cognitive style		
'Holistic' learning style (Pask, 1973)	•	Uses a global approach to problem solving
	•	Personalises learning
	•	Uses individual 'props' to aid understanding
	•	Needs overall picture as a guide to learning right from the start - fits in details much later on
	•	Needs to "work ahead", to get an overview of the topic as a whole from the start
Intuitive thinker	•	Part of the process of holistic thinking - 'knows' the answer through making associations and personal knowledge or thought, rather than systematic working out.
Strong visual-spatial thinker	•	Can use "*a form of thought in which images are generated or recalled in the mind and are manipulated, overlaid, translated, associated with other similar forms. They can be rotated, increased or reduced in size, distorted, or otherwise transformed gradually from one familiar image into another.*" (Thomas G West)
	•	Responds to visual-spatial patterns, eg keyboard
Concrete learner	•	Sometimes needs to feel materials before writing or reading about the topic or try something out
	•	Good at 'hands on' practical skills
	•	Learns better from actively investigating subject rather than passively sitting back and hearing the information from teacher
Divergent thinker	•	Makes connections between many different concepts and can see the interrelationship between sometimes unconnected ideas
Inductive thinker	•	Learns from lots of experience and practice rather than generalisations and rules
Good spatial thinker	•	Can use three dimensional space creatively (eg architects, engineers)

Right brained dyslexic people

Visual thinking - an intellectual strength!

GENIUS	Experience of difficulties with linguistic coding
Michael Faraday	All had difficulties in early schooling. All found school work which entailed high verbal skills, especially reading and writing, particularly difficult.
Thomas Edison	
Albert Einstein	Einstein had difficulties with arithmetic.
General George Patton	All were considered 'slow' learners when young.
William Butler Yeats	All thought in pictures and utilised their highly visual mode to advantage. Some found it difficult to translate the whole image to the written word (eg Einstein) although the visual mode helped the written word in the case of dyslexic writers.
Hans Christian Anderson	
Winston Churchill	None became good spellers and many continued to have difficulties with punctuation.
Woodrow Wilson	
Leonardo Da Vinci	Leonardo thought in pictures first - then had to deconstruct the image into writing (which he did back to front).

Why do dyslexic people rely more on right hemisphere processing?

Some writers argue that dyslexic people have achieved greatness not in spite of but because of their dyslexia. In our literate world a lack of automaticity in literacy is regarded as a problem and often impedes progress in work and education. However, it can be argued that this 'weakness' may be seen **as a manifestation of a strength in a different mode of thought.**

> *"It has become increasingly clear in recent years that dyslexics themselves are frequently endowed with high talents in many areas......... Moreover, the notion of 'special abilities' is supported by its prevalence."*
> (Geschwind in an address to the Orton Dyslexia Society in 1982)

Galaburda (another neurologist), observed microscopic lesions (areas of damage or diminished growth, usually in the left hemisphere) and unusual symmetry of certain formations in the dyslexic brain. He therefore postulated the theory that these lesions, whilst suppressing the development of some areas of the

"I made a writing desk while everyone else in the class was struggling over basic carpentry joints"

The Dyslexic Learning Style

> "I can work from plans because I have a kind of 3D mind - I can get inside something just from looking at a plan"

> "I'm good at internal things like combustion engines and I can see principles of engineering"

brain actually increase the development of others. For instance, many dyslexic people have developed a highly visual mode of thinking, to the extent of being able to plan complex three dimensional designs and plans totally within their thoughts.

"Does the facility for visual-spatial thinking (primarily a right brain function), preclude the use of the left? The dichotomy is perhaps not so extreme and of course many successful dyslexic and non-dyslexic people function inter-hemispherically. The whole brain is actively participating in perception, encoding of information, organisation of representations, memory, arousal, planning, thinking and understanding...."
(Levy, J. 1985).

> "I have trouble remembering letters on a dial phone - I have to draw a keypad and remember how I tap it out and then write down the number"

However, there is some suggestion of the connection between processing weaknesses in the left hemisphere, and more highly developed skills in right hemispheric functioning. Current brain research suggests that dyslexic brains are differently organised, or that dyslexic people may use different parts of their brains than non-dyslexic people for at least some activities. (see *Neurological Perspective*)

> "I can't read music but I see music in patterns - shapes like triangles and rectangles"

Why is it important to understand the dyslexic learning style?

In most cases, approximately 90 per cent of traditional classroom instruction is geared to the auditory-verbal learner (Dunn and Dunn, 1986). Teachers talk to their students, ask questions, expect responses. It is difficult not to accept the notion that many teachers favour the left hemisphere approach in the classroom (Kolb, 1984). Dyslexic students are disadvantaged in such an environment, as they cannot absorb and respond to linguistic information quickly or automatically.

Understanding differences in learning style encourages teachers to adapt their teaching to meet the needs of the students, by perhaps talking less and using more active learning approaches. Motivation as well as learning can be improved through the use of global, visual-spatial, concrete or 'hands on' and developing personalised strategies for learning.

In addition, individual perceptual-motor strengths and weaknesses can be addressed in helping learners find effective strategies for remembering and accessing verbal information. This leads to not only more success, but more autonomy in learning. In addressing the learning style of dyslexic students, individuality in learning can be better taken into account and all

The Dyslexic Learning Style

students can benefit.

Careers advisers and employers also need to be aware of the positive gifts and potential of the dyslexic cognitive style so that dyslexic young people and adults do not continue to fail and underachieve but have more opportunity to contribute fully and even to excel.

As Thomas G West says,

> "…the conventional education system may be focussing on the wrong kind of skills and on rewarding some of the wrong kinds of learning. Conventional education practices may be substantially weeding out many of those who might have the most to give."

What do these people have in common?

- Michaelangelo — artist
- Woodrow Wilson — former President US
- Don McMullen — photographer
- Michael Heseltine — politician
- Linda La Plante — TV writer
- Richard Rogers — architect
- Duncan Goodhew — swimmer
- August Rodin — sculptor
- Cher — actress & singer
- W B Yeats — poet
- Winston Churchill — former Prime Minister
- Thomas Edison — inventor of the light bulb
- Whoopi Goldberg — actress
- Albert Einstein — scientist
- General George Patton — US Army
- Jacky Stewart — racing driver
- James Whale — TV presenter
- Tom Cruise — actor
- Liza Cody — writer
- Michael Faraday — scientist
- Hans Christian Andersen — writer

They are all dyslexic!

III Theoretical Perspectives

Neuropsychological perspective

*"This is a medical problems with a neurological basis.
It's not the fault of the child, the parents or the schools."
(Dr. Paula Tallal, Centre for Molecular and Behavioural Neuroscience, Rutgers University)*

The difficulties which dyslexic people experience with language processing vary from person to person. Some find it difficult to distinguish or retain sounds, others have great difficulties with 'seeing' print or recognising words, while others have difficulties when attempting to put pen to paper or in the act of handwriting itself; many have all of these difficulties to some degree. If one studies the various definitions of dyslexia, irrespective of which modality is argued as being responsible for the condition, all agree that the condition affects the processing of written language. Such linguistic functions are all dependent on the brain. Therefore when examining the condition of dyslexia, it is impossible to ignore the neurological aspects.

Neuropsychology is the study of brain behaviour. Dyslexia can be seen as a neuropsychological condition, studied in terms of how the brain processes language and how the 'by-products' of language, for example reading and writing, are affected when a dysfunction occurs. Both experimental and clinical investigation of dyslexia have emphasised the neuropsychological bases of the disorder. Examining dyslexia from this perspective can shed light on how the brain is organised to deal with the complex integration required for any linguistic task.

Developmental dyslexia is the name given to the condition whereby children may be born with a language dysfunction or suffer some developmental delay in processing language and acquiring written language skills. In developmental dyslexia, there are no 'hard' neurological signs of damage.

Understanding of the functions of various language centres in the brain has come in large part from studies of **acquired dyslexia** which is a term to describe the situation when existing reading or writing skills are lost because of a stroke or some other major accident.

Language (signing is included in this category) is central to any human's development; socially, intellectually and academically. Different research into different parts of the brain sheds light on the possible inhibitors to efficient and thus speedy processing of linguistic information.

Functions of the human brain

The brain is divided into four main lobes, each with a specialised function: the frontal, the parietal, occipital and temporal lobes.

1. **The frontal lobe** is primarily involved with higher-level processes such as planning, intellectual synthesis and understanding of moral behaviour.

    The motor cortex, *important in co-ordinating fine hand, finger and facial as well as other body movements is also found in this area. The motor strip appears to integrate input concerned with spatial synthesis (right brain), language (left brain) and tactile-kinaesthetic communication (right brain).* (See figure a)

2. **The temporal lobe** is mainly concerned with sensory reception for hearing and certain higher mental processes such as memory.

    The left temporal lobe (in the left hemisphere) is also concerned with the analysis and synthesis of sounds of speech, understanding speech, naming of objects (also a function of the left parietal lobe), the recall of words and sequencing. (see figure a)

    The right temporal lobe (in the right hemisphere) is involved in remembering non-verbal material for example faces, abstract patterns or maze learning.

3. **The parietal lobe** constitutes the primary body sense area which detects pain, touch, cold, heat and the feeling of bodily movement. The somatosensory cortex which facilitates sensitivity in the areas of the body is found in the parietal lobe. (see figure a)

    This area also organises complex simultaneous spatial syntheses such as telling the time by hand positions on a clock or finding bearing on a map. Within the left hemisphere, the parietal lobe is also important in language skills such as organising logical grammatical structures (as opposed to narrative speech) and the naming of objects. The right parietal lobe is particularly important for visuospatial skills.

4. **The occipital lobe** is mainly concerned with visual reception and the processing of visual memory. (see figure a)

Theoretical Perspectives

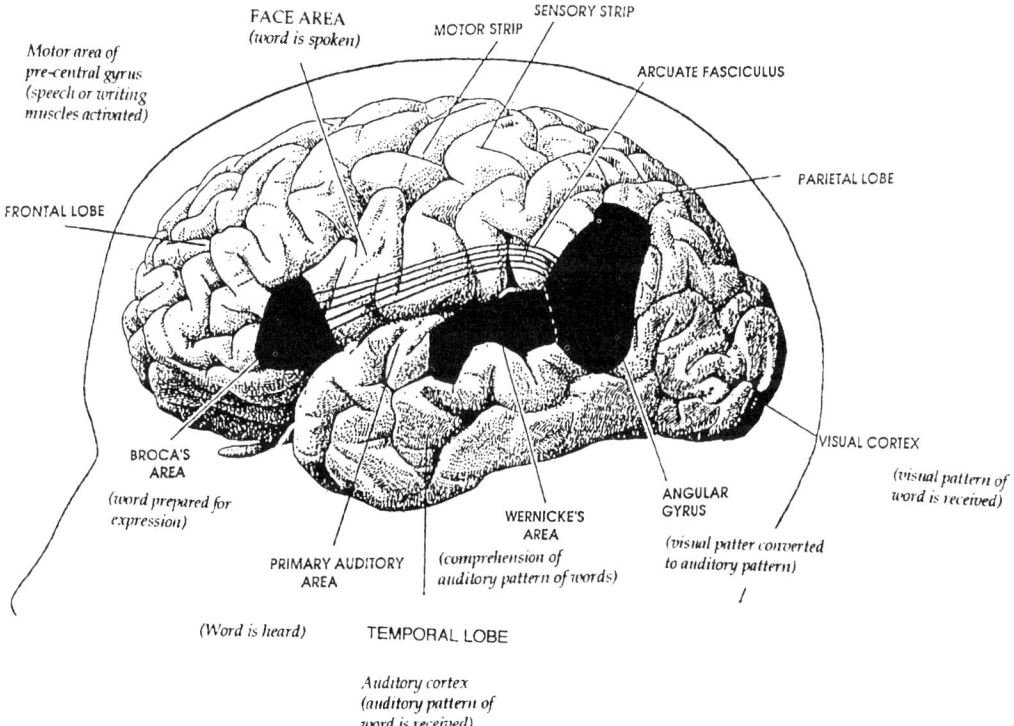

fig a (courtesy of Dr John F Stein)

The term cortex (from the Latin meaning bark) is used to refer to the outer layer of cells. The motor and somatosensory cortex are important areas of the brain for integration of functions which are needed for reading, writing and spelling. (see fig b)

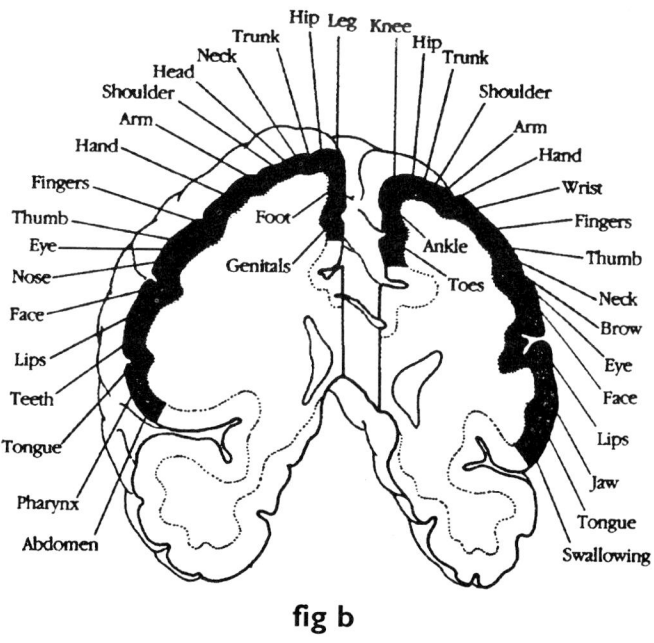

fig b

from: **'Brain function and blood flow'** by Niels A. Lassen, David H. Ingvar and Erik Shinhøj October 1978 © Scientific American all rights reserved.

Lateralisation

The brain is divided into two hemispheres - the left hemisphere and the right hemisphere. Each hemisphere is organised to specialise in certain functions so that processing of various actions or tasks takes less time and is thus more efficient. This hemispherical organisation of specialist functioning is known as **cerebral dominance.** Lateralisation is the process whereby functions come to be located primarily on one side of the brain. The brain operates cross-laterally; thus the left part of the brain controls the right side of the body and vice versa. When we examine laterality, we not only examine which side of the brain controls which functions, but also whether messages are transmitted to the appropriate side of the body. For instance, in order to process language, it is convenient for the brain if the right ear is dominant so information can quickly be sent to the appropriate language areas in the left hemisphere for speedy processing.

Cerebral dominance is related to lateral dominance, which can be seen in the case of handedness. Very few people are ambidextrous, indicating they have internalised a preference for one hemisphere over the other. However, laterality is relative, not absolute, as both hemispheres play a role in nearly every behaviour. Although the left hemisphere is especially important for the production of language, the right hemisphere also has some language capabilities, but has no ability to analyse speech sounds.

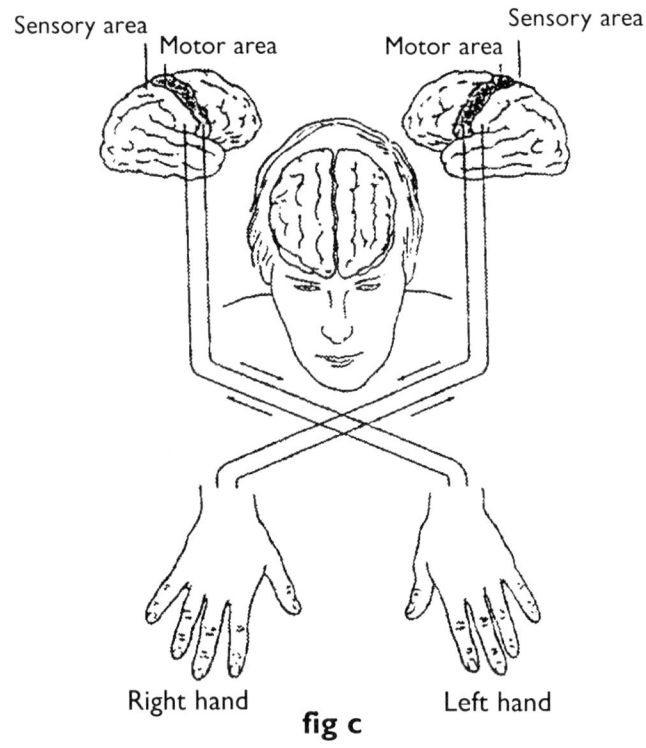

fig c

from: **Left Brain, Right Brain** © Springer and Deutsch 3rd edition 1989 used with permission of W H Freeman & Co.

Theoretical Perspectives

The two hemispheres of the brain are cross-connected by a thick nerve cable composed of millions of fibres which allow transmission of information between the two hemispheres. This linking cable is called the **corpus collosum.** The corpus collosum enables messages from the left side of the body to be sent to the right hemisphere of the brain and vice versa.

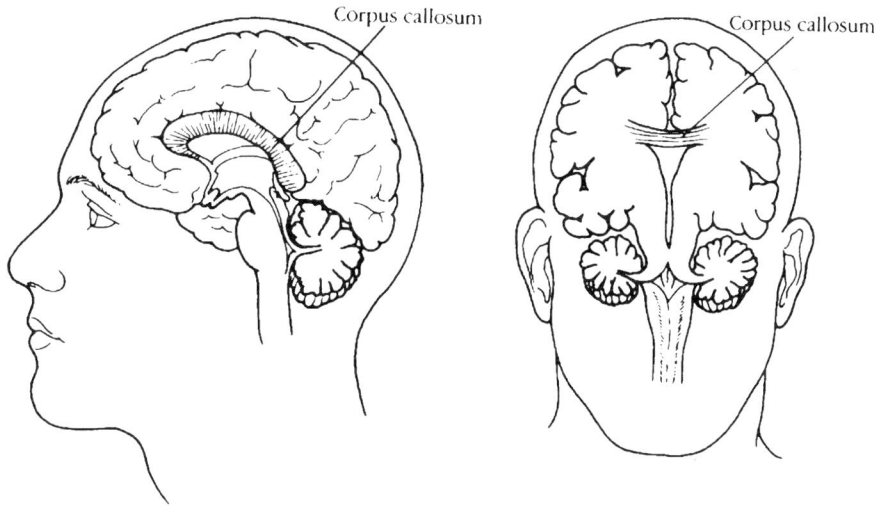

fig d

from: **Left Brain, Right Brain** © Springer and Deutsch 2nd edition 1989 used with permission of W H Freeman & Co.

Due to the specialised functions in the left and right brain, human brains are normally **asymmetrical.** As the language function is very important to humans, the language areas in the left hemisphere are more developed. The research conducted by Roger Sperry of 'split brain' patients involved the severing of the corpus collosum to stop epileptic seizures. Although successful in stopping the epileptic seizures, the resultant observation of the patients provided insights into the individual workings of the two hemispheres: *"...there appear[ed] to be two modes of thinking, verbal and non-verbal, represented rather separately in left and right hemispheres..."* (Sperry, 1973). The mode of thinking in the left hemisphere was verbal, analytical, sequential and logical, whereas the mode of the right hemisphere specialised more in visuo-spatial, global creative thinking.

Evidence suggests (Bakker, 1976) that the dyslexic brain tends to be more symmetrical than the normal brain and is therefore less efficient in processing language. In such cases, both sides of the brain may be competing to handle language and there is less preference or specialisation for reception or output of language based tasks. Due to this lack of specialist functioning, any processing of language appears to take longer as the brain may be subject to confusions due to messages having to keep crossing hemispheres.

However, this anomaly does not affect other areas of the brain where cognition, thought or creativity occur. In fact, as the right hemisphere has compensated for the deficit in processing literacy skills, there may be a superior development of cortical regions mediating other functions, particularly visuo-spatial skills which are not language based,

> " ... many dyslexics have superior talents in certain areas of non-verbal skill, such as art, architecture, engineering and athletics. The immediate naive presumption is that success in these fields is simply the result of compensatory achievement in non-verbal fields on the part of those who do not succeed in readily acquiring reading. I believe that this explanation must convey at best a very small fraction of the truth."
> (Geschwind, 1982).

Language and Speech

The earliest identification of language disorders was made by doctors such as Paul Broca (1860s) and Karl Wernicke (1874) who conducted post-mortem examinations on patients suffering brain damage after a stroke. Their research showed that the main language centres of the brain in most people are located in the left hemisphere.

Broca discovered that patients who lost the facility for **expressive** speech (aphemia, motor or expressive aphasia) were damaged in a particular area of the left brain, now know as **Broca's area**. He also found that if the lesions occurred on the corresponding area in the right hemisphere, the patient retained the power of speech and communication although activities such as singing were sometimes affected. (see fig a)

Similarly, Wernicke discovered that certain of his patients after suffering a stroke could still articulate speech, but could not understand what was said to them and their spoken communication became meaningless. The patients in this category, when examined at autopsy, had developed lesions in the area of the brain now known as **Wernicke's area**. People affected in this area suffer from sensory or **receptive aphasia**.

In 1891 Dejerine performed post mortem examinations on patients with acquired **alexia** (loss of reading) and **agraphia** (loss of writing skill), but retained their capacity for verbal speech and comprehension. The damage in these cases was shown to be at the junction of the temporal, parietal and occipital lobes in the left brain, where the language centres are located.

Difficulties with visual processing and perception

Since the nineteenth century there has been a recognition that there exists a relationship between deficits in visual processing and difficulties with reading, although there has been much controversy about this view. Research by Stein, Fowler and Lovegrove has now shown that dyslexic children and adults tend to have a weakness in the magnocellular transient subsystem of the retina when attempting to read.

The visual system has two sub-systems which carry information to the visual cortex - the transient system and the sustained system. The magnocellular (transient) system is the first to respond to a stimulus and relies on further detail from the parvocellular (sustained) system. The differences between the two systems is briefly described below:

TRANSIENT *(magnocellular)*	**SUSTAINED** *(parvocellular)*
highly sensitive to contrast	low sensitivity to contrast
sensitive to large stimuli	sensitive to small stimuli
peripheral vision	central vision
has a fast transmission	has a slow transmission
able to change rapidly	changes slowly

The 'transient' (magnocellular) system is vital to the *timing* of visual stimuli, and plays an important part in detecting the movement of objects *"and ultimately their signals are used to control eye and limb movements made in relation to visual targets"* (Stein, 1991). Lovegrove (1991) in his research showed that dyslexic children had a much reduced sensitivity of the transient system compared to non-dyslexic children. This has the result of slowing down the visual processing system and causing unstable binocular control and inaccurate judgements of visual direction, and *"....hence their tendency to superimpose letters on top of each other, and missequence letters in a word."* The work of Dr John Stein and Dr Susan Fowler at Oxford University has involved extensive research into the difficulties caused by unstable vergence eye-movement control (ie a lack of reference eye). Children with whom they were working complained that *"letters and words appear to move around, jump over each other, blur and reverse themselves".*

The lack of a reference eye may cause serious problems when trying to read. In visual perception the eyes normally act independently to give us a sense of depth, but when reading, we need to fixate on a stable and unified image to make sense of letters and words. Because of our binocular vision, to avoid a 'double image', the brain only perceives the image of the reference eye. In many dyslexic children the brain has not 'decided' on a reference eye and this impedes perception of a stable image. Reading may well require that information from the magnocellular system and the parvocellular system be differently synchronised at particular stages in visual information processing. (Pumfrey, 1993).

A common complaint by many students is that the print does not hold steady on the page. The occurrence and type of print instability varies from student to student - for some it blurs, for others it moves on the page or jumps out at the student, or even forms circular whirls or rivers of print on the page. Such a phenomenon has been called scotopic sensitivity syndrome or SSS (Irlen, 1991).

Sufferers from scotopic sensitivity syndrome may experience light sensitivity or have inadequate background accommodation, whereby the white of the paper and the black of the print vie for dominance. Often the white wins out, and the print becomes indistinguishable from the page. Other students report that the print jumps or shakes on the page and sometimes it falls off the page.

Another difficulty experienced by students with SSS is a restricted fixation span. In the case of most readers, when a reading burst is launched, the eye lands on the words within a phrase and when the eye has gathered enough information, pauses until it re-fixates and launches into another saccade. A saccade is the term used to describe the rapid jerk by which an eye moves across a line of print. A saccade lasts between a fiftieth and twentieth of a second. (Ellis, 1984). The launches into the saccades are normally done quickly, automatically and smoothly. However, any difficulties with eye pulsations means that the saccadic control is disturbed and thus information cannot be loaded into the processing areas of the brain for comprehension to occur. Poorer readers have too many launches, begin too many saccades and reading often becomes 'word for word'. As people with such a processing difficulty cannot 'land' smoothly when attempting to launch a saccade, the tracking of print is difficult and readers often fail to gain 'cohesion' from the text which necessitates backward and forward tracking.

Difficulties with auditory processing and perception

Auditory perception does not refer to hearing acuity problems, but deals with how the brain codes and discriminates phonological information in order to process speech, carry out memory tasks and make sense of phonemes when attempting to put sounds to spelling or reading. Many dyslexic students have difficulties with such phonological processing.

Most auditory processing (especially in non-dyslexics) occurs in the left hemisphere which is specialised for speech and language. One explanation offered for poor phonological processing is that the language areas in the brain are organised in a more symmetrical way with less linguistic specialisation in the left hemisphere, making it difficult for automatic processing of phonological information to occur. Another is that there was a delay or interference in maturation, possibly due to glue ear at a crucial stage in development of auditory discriminating and acquisition of speech sounds.

The latest research from America, headed by Dr Paula Tallal (1994), suggests that dyslexia is not specifically a visual or ordinary hearing problem, but maybe a flaw in a specific brain circuit that handles rapidly flowing auditory information. The study found that the left brain hemispheres of dyslexic children had fewer cells of the kind that specialise in comprehending rapid sounds and this led to comprehension difficulties and in learning to read. These difficulties began in infancy whereby the children could not hear many of the components of ordinary language, especially blends where the change in sound is too quick for the dyslexic child to perceive.

The non-dyslexic reader may have better access to internalising and interpreting speech sounds because of the greater development of the language areas which are predominantly in the left hemisphere. They are therefore better able to develop meta-linguistic skills of rhyming, phonological segmentation and discrimination. Discriminating the subtleties of sound is important to any linguistic task, as is the ability to hold these sounds in the short term memory. Tasks such as reading and spelling require good auditory perceptual skills and an ability to hold these items within the short term memory.

The brain does not, however, deal in isolated and integral units. Each area of the brain whether specialising in processing language based tasks or not, must interrelate and send messages to other parts of the brain; this is especially evident in complex tasks such as reading and writing. Norman Geschwind's early premise was that the **angular gyrus** plays a major role in the formation of associations between vision and audition - a crucial interrelationship involved in reading. Lesions in the angular gyrus have the effect of disconnecting the visual and auditory systems which affect reading and writing adversely.

The ongoing work of Geschwind and Galaburda (1984) showed the existence of physical, structural alteration in some dyslexic brains. Galaburda's work concentrated on micro-anatomical studies of the brains of deceased adult dyslexics, whereby he discovered microscopic lesions in the area of the **planum temporale,** which is part of the primary auditory cortex. Geschwind has pointed to the correlation between the delay in the acquisition of speech in dyslexic children (first mooted by Orton as early as 1925) which would indicate " ... *a delay in the development of the entire system devoted to language.*" Geschwind (1982) also posited the theory that as the language system in the left hemisphere is weak, dyslexic people often develop remarkable strengths in the right hemisphere.

What causes dyslexia?

In cases of developmental dyslexia, it is thought that small lesions found in the left hemisphere, may be congenital or have followed a mild childhood seizure or minor damage at birth. (Many such lesions heal throughout childhood but may result in a developmental lag, especially in reading and writing).

Another discovery has shown that when lesions have formed at the pre-natal stage the foetus may develop a corresponding language centre in the right hemisphere of the brain and in some other cortical regions. There is some slight evidence supporting the theory that in dyslexic children with symmetrical hemispheres the foetus was attacked by a 'disorder of the immune system'. The pregnant mother may have been subject to an allergy or suffered a virus during the first three months of pregnancy. Obviously, not all mothers who have a virus during this vulnerable stage of foetal development will give birth to dyslexic children, but it is possible that some congenital developmental dyslexia may be attributed to such a cause.

Other research notes a maturational lag caused by slower development of the nerve fibres of the **corpus collosum.** The process of nerve fibre maturation is called **myelination.** The corpus collosum myelinates rapidly between the ages of two and seven (this can vary significantly in individuals), while some nerve fibres develop even up to the age of 12. If these fibres linking the two hemispheres together are delayed in growth, affected children are not physiologically capable of tasks which require hemispheric integration. This may later cause a difficulty with the two hemispheres competing for information or language functions not being adequately specialised.

Dyslexia can also be hereditary, and there is strong evidence that there is a genetically determined predisposition in certain families. Hallgren (1950) in his study of 112 Swedish families, found that 88% of dyslexics had others in their family who were similarly affected. Other later studies have confirmed this correlation. Pennington and Smith (1983) give an overview of the several studies conducted:

> *"Some forms of dyslexia are transmitted genetically and there are likely to be several forms of familial dyslexia involving different modes of transmission. Dyslexia does not appear to be a sex-linked disorder. but there is a sex difference in expression, likely due in part to normal, genetically based sex differences in language skills".*

The difficulties which beset dyslexic students in writing, spelling and reading cannot be inherited but there may be some underlying inherited cognitive or neurological organisational difference which may result in difficulties with processing language. However, the knowledge that there may be such a basis for these difficulties does not mean that such difficulties are fixed and such students destined for academic failure. Indeed, an understanding of how the brain is organised provides a framework upon which to structure the most appropriate teaching methods and strategies to meet an individual's learning style.

New Horizons

Currently, new techniques of computerised x-ray tomography (CAT), magnetic resonance imaging (MRI) and positron emission tomography (PET) are used as valuable clinical tools for the detection of brain dynamics and abnormalities in the living person. They are now used routinely in scientific studies of brain functions. This is particularly useful to those neuropsychologists studying dyslexia as they can now work with the living. Ironically, many of these 'high tech' computers using colour coded topographical mapping methods, simply confirm research conducted in the 19th century by doctors such as Broca, Wernicke and Dejerine, who tested their hypotheses through post-mortem examinations!

However, even more highly developed techniques are expected during this last decade of the 20th century - in America, declared "The Decade of the Brain". Research is now able to give us detailed images inside the 'hidden black box' - the brain - and these scanning techniques enable scientists to see what is happening at the very moment a person is reading or writing.

Exciting new research in Britain (not yet published) is currently being undertaken by Dr. Uta Frith, working with an inter-disciplinary team who use brain scanning techniques to examine different patterns of relative brain activity in dyslexic adults. Her research model aims to integrate the biological basis of dyslexia to the cognitive aspects and environmental factors which affect the individual within the spheres of education, work and life.

Theoretical Perspectives

Cognitive perspective

"All cognition is recognition"
(Plato)

Cognitive psychology is concerned with issues of perception, awareness, memory, thought and motivation. All these areas of 'cognition' or knowledge have an integral effect on how we learn and are therefore of importance in understanding difficulties which dyslexic students experience in reading, spelling and writing.

Our cognitive development is part of the normal maturation process of human development. Without cognition, humans would not be able to learn either simple skills or the more complex ones of reading and writing. By the time children are seven, their cognitive style is nearly matured. Exploring cognitive differences between dyslexic and non-dyslexic subjects can shed light on dyslexia as an 'alternative cognitive style'. Psychologists have concentrated on various aspects of cognition in studying dyslexia, primarily the processes underlying reading and spelling.

Cognitive models of language processing

What is often missing in the medical literature which deals with dyslexia is an applied methodology for analysing the nature of the process whereby individuals learn to read and write. In particular, they do not detail how we process alphabetic or syllabic symbols which have to be initially perceived visually or auditorily and then transformed within the cognitive areas of the brain into linguistic sense and meaning.

Reading has always occupied a central place within cognitive psychology. A cognitive approach to reading and spelling disabilities emphasises the mental functions which are involved in these tasks and attempts to pin-point areas of disturbance.

The traditional research tool of the cognitive psychologist has been the controlled experiment. In order that the many psychological process which make reading and writing possible may be studied, cognitive psychologists sometimes organise theoretical models to explain how this transmission occurs. Such models often take the form of flow-chart diagrams. They attempt to show the stages through which information is relayed in order that meaning is gained or the reading and writing process enacted.

The cognitive model shown below depicts a theoretical reading system which has been simplified in order to show us the complex psycho-linguistic tasks involved in reading the word 'cat' aloud. It shows two routes to reading, direct and indirect. The direct, or visual recognition route is the route the skilled reader uses. It is rapid and relies on an internal lexicon. The indirect or phonic mediation route is used by skilled readers for decoding unfamiliar words and checking accuracy, and by learners for developing word attack and internalising the alphabetic system. It is clear from the diagram that the direct route is much quicker.

Model of single word processing using both visual and auditory routes

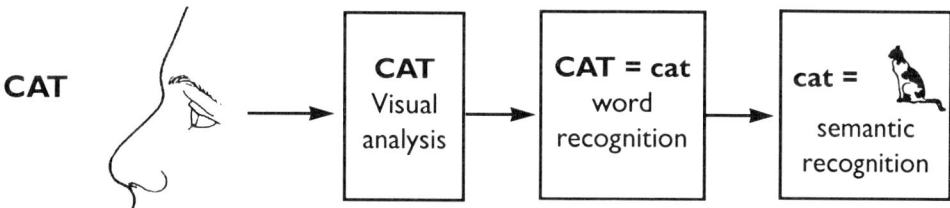

Model of direct route to reading

(visual recognition/sight vocabulary)

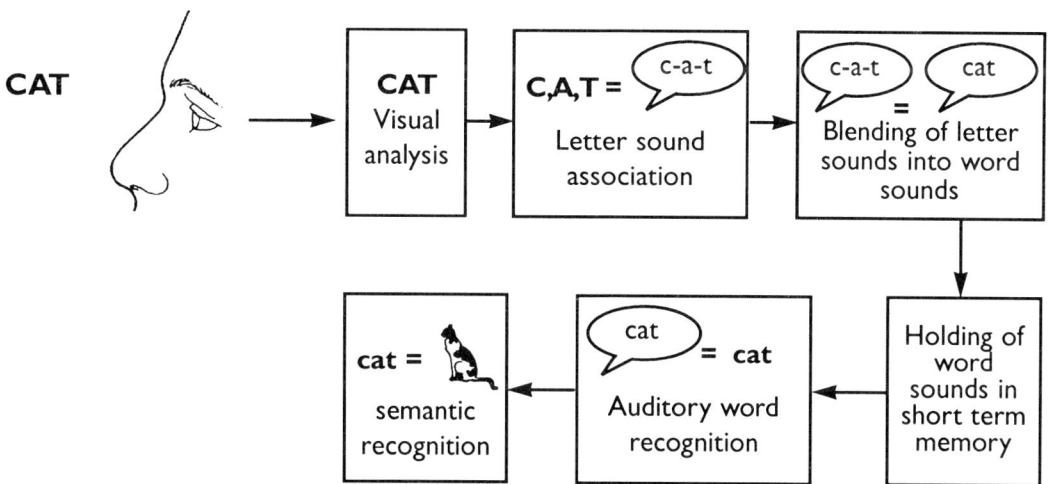

Model of indirect route to reading

(phonic mediation)

If difficulties are experienced with the direct visual route and the indirect phonic route is used, readers will find reading slower and more likely to interfere with understanding, as there are many more steps involved in using the indirect route.

Those with problems using the indirect route find it hard to master the sound-symbol system and to decode new words. Although they can use the direct route, they will not be able to check accuracy through phonological analysis or to read words they do not recognise.

Dyslexic readers may experience difficulties with one or the other, or sometimes both, routes in accessing meaning from print.

One advantage of such theoretical models is that the diagrammatic operations enable us to understand where the specific difficulties in processing can occur. They therefore broaden understanding of the problems and point to strategies which can best be used to compensate for difficulties.

Memory

Cognition involves memory, and dyslexic learners have problems with **short term** or '**working**' memory. Because of the weaknesses in coding linguistic information, dyslexic learners rely on **long-term memory**, which involves association of ideas and understanding.

Memory is crucial in any learning task, but the brain must first process incoming information in the short term memory. Short term memory can be said to be a *"a subset of processes which enables the working memory to function"* (Baddeley, 1986). Long-term memory refers to a relatively durable store, holding information for indefinate periods of time, some lasting a lifetime. The two important components of long term memory are the episodic memory (memory of one's personal life) and semantic memory (memory for everyday objects and activities such as speaking or knowing what words mean).

The processes of reading and writing necessitate efficient use of visual and auditory short term memories - which 'hold' visual or auditory information for subsequent encoding and storing in the long term memory, or for the immediate execution of tasks such as remembering a phone number while dialling or copying information from a board. In verbal tasks, information is generally coded and rehearsed in the auditory short-term memory, whose role is to hold sequentially arriving units of information for long enough for the user to use or apply the information given. Many dyslexic learners show poor phonological perception, including weak discrimination, segmentation or blending of sounds which affects efficient processing within the auditory memory. They also show weaknesses in 'chunking', or grouping words and letters when needing to learn words to read or to spell.

Most people can hold five to nine items or 'chunks' in their short-term memory. Being able to chunk thus increases the capacity of the short-term memory. For instance, the alphabet is usually taught in chunks (*eg abcd efg hijk, etc*) as this enables the learner to memorise seven chunks of letters, instead of 28 individual letters. Lack of ability to chunk therefore increases the load on the short-term memory and contributes to dyslexic learners' problems with memorising.

Initial input into the short-term memory comes from the senses; we see, we hear, we feel, we touch. However, our processing of such information into the long-term memory relies on **coding strategies** for storing information in the long term memory. Strategies are also needed to retrieve information from the long term memory. Dyslexic people tend to show weaknesses in visual and/or phonological coding which hinders their ability to memorise information. Consequently, they tend to rely on **semantic** memory, or meaning in order to remember. Dyslexic people remember best when they use meaningful associations for memorising and can make personal sense of what they are learning.

Interaction between memory systems

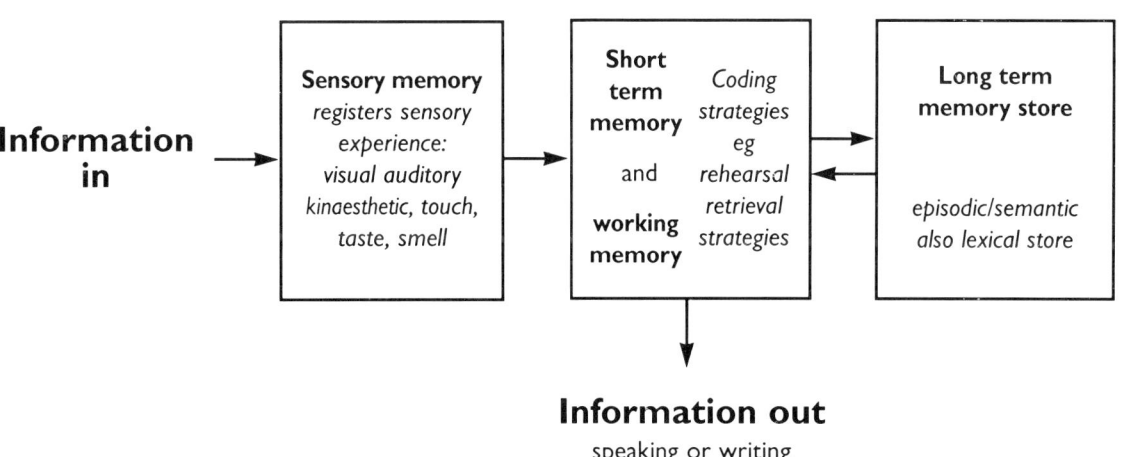

Baddeley's team (1986) concentrated their research on a more dynamic model of memory, whereby **the working memory** has an active processing function, not merely one of passive storage of information. In Baddeley's model, both the 'holding' (STM or short term memory) and processing functions (working memory) compete for limited 'storage' capacity, but if an individual can integrate both these two functions then the processing of linguistic information will be quicker and more efficient and accurate. Baddeley's model operates on the premise that working memory has three components: a **central executive**, which is the control system which selects and operates various processes; the **articulatory loop**, which specialises in sub-vocal rehearsal and verbal storage and the **visuo-spatial 'scratch-pad'** which specialises in imagery and spatial memory.

Theoretical Perspectives

The articulatory loop inputs and codes verbal information, the scratch-pad codes visual information. However, the working memory also acts as a buffer for already 'neatly' coded information. Dyslexic people often have a very good long-term memory but sometimes find it difficult to hold and retrieve information quickly and efficiently for use in writing tasks.

Baddeley's model of working memory indicates that if the transfer of information is incomplete due to verbal or orthographic encoding or decoding difficulties then the working memory becomes less efficient at passing the information along to the long-term memory. Instead, it must use some of its capacity to decode the input from either or both of the peripheral systems (ie the articulatory loop or the visuo-spatial scratch pad) and thereby has less capacity or energy left over for other activities.

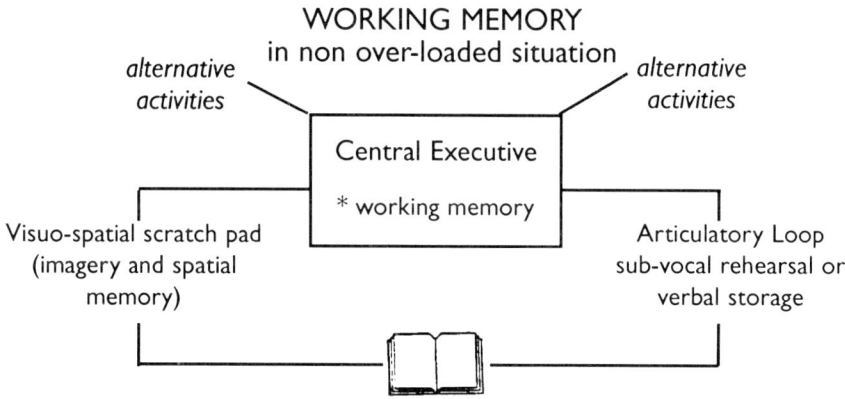

Key   Free information flow from peripheral systems of short-term memory to working memory

*   able to process information systems into long-term memory

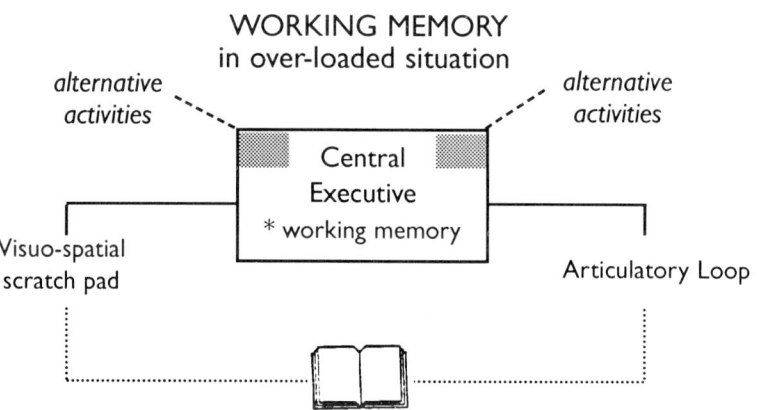

Key

.... peripheral systems over-loaded (cannot cope with tasks)

▓▓▓▓ area devoted to storage to compensate for weakness in peripheral system

------- limited resources available for alternative activities - restricted access to long term memory (adapted from Alan Baddeley)

Phonological Coding

As can be seen from the Baddeley model of working memory, the auditory loop is important for verbal storage and rehearsal. It is therefore important that a person's auditory perception be adequate to encode, decode and store the codes of language necessary for linguistic tasks. Auditory perception does not refer to hearing acuity but the ability to *discriminate* and *process* sounds that are heard.

Dr Margaret Snowling (1987) puts forward a model of acoustic analysis, whereby the skills of sound blending, phonemic awareness and semantic memory are integrated components which enable language based tasks to occur. Her model examines the relationship between spoken and written language processing systems and relates to Frith's model of reading acquisition. Snowling argues that young children have a stored visual lexicon which is linked to a semantic memory store. This in turn is linked to a phonological output which enables pronunciation of these known words. The words in this sight vocabulary are recognised and spoken automatically, but as the demands of reading increase, children come across unknown and perhaps more sophisticated words which they need to decipher. In order to decode these new words, children have to develop the letter-sound relationships, classified by Frith as components of the 'alphabetic phase' (see Developmental Perspective).

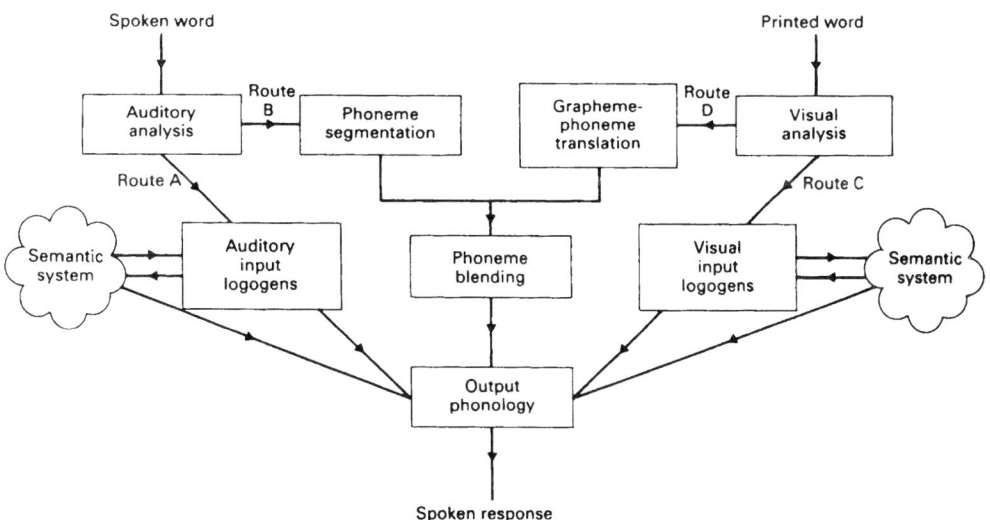

Model of the interface between spoken and written language processing system
(with permission from Dr M Snowling)

Snowling's model simplifies the processing routes necessary for language. We see that the 'look and say' route to accessing meaning from print is marked as Route C. Unfamiliar words, or multi-syllabic words would be processed primarily through route D. The spoken word is processed by routes A and B.

Theoretical Perspectives

Snowling points to evidence which shows phonemic deficits both at the level of speech perception, verbal naming, verbal memory and in written language skills. A dyslexic student with poor auditory perception may have difficulty in processing speech during lectures or when given instructions for the completion of a task or spelling words out during note-taking due to inefficient phonological segmentation skills. These segmentation skills are important in listening as they constitute an ability to hold items within the short-term memory for tasks such as taking notes and for processing information into the long term memory. When spelling, a person must not only perceive sound syllables of multi-syllabic words, but also retain them for the duration of writing that word. Many dyslexic people are unable to hold the necessary information in order to produce a word. Studies have shown that memory difficulties occur among dyslexic persons in tasks demanding rapid auditory processing. It is thought this is a result of a limited capacity for rehearsal due to poor phonological coding skills.

Verbal naming is another aspect of phonological coding which dyslexic people have difficulties with. This is aptly demonstrated in Snowling's case study of Jackie. Jackie was better at remembering items presented through a visual modality rather than a purely auditory one. However, when presented with a word naming task (The Boston Naming Test) which required a picture to be named, she could not 'find' the exact word, making errors of circumlocutions (long, drawn-out explanations): (*pyramid* became "*an Egyptian grave thing*"), as well as articulation (*hor-sea-uh* for *seahorse*). In the majority of cases the circumlocutions were semantically correct showing knowledge of the deep semantic structures but an inability to spontaneously find and articulate the correct word.

Further evidence of Jackie's verbal difficulties were shown when she was asked to describe a picture. The account was inarticulate and hesitant, with gestures used to convey meaning where ever possible. She also had difficulties with discriminating sounds, and words and was slower in rhyming than others in her age group. Dr Snowling concludes that

> "... Jackie was subject to a variety of verbal deficits. It could be argued that it was these which placed her at a disadvantage in learning to read and to spell..."

Indeed, many dyslexic adolescents and adults who have difficulties with written language often remark that they are constantly frustrated by knowing what they want to say, but not being able to "get it out"!

The cognitive perceptive is a valuable tool for examining dyslexia, as the varying models of language processing help us understand why learning, or reading and writing have been inhibited.

Developmental Perspective

Every child enters school expecting to learn to read. Those who make reasonable progress are well on their way to a successful school career. Those who do not, experience disappointment in school and in themselves as students.... But without reading, what is their future - academic or otherwise?
(Marilyn Jager Adams 1993)

The developmental perspective of dyslexia is an aspect of the cognitive approach with an emphasis on how language skills develop in the maturing child and the difficulties which may occur if these skills fail to develop normally.

All children, whatever their differences, come into a world of language. This linguistic world is constituted by a complex interplay of neurological functions, physiological factors, cultural and social expectations and the linguistic rules and constructs of that particular language. The patterns of individual language development are aptly described by Vygotsky (1934) as a series of stages at which *"thought becomes verbal, and speech becomes rational"*.

Most children learn this process of language acquisition quickly, easily, naturally. Some have severe difficulties acquiring speech and language; these are dysphasic (***dys***= faulty: ***phasis*** = speech). Others show weaknesses in linguistic skills which manifest themselves primarily in reading and writing. Those children (and adults) who are poor with words (ie dyslexic) will perform less well than their peer group in linguistic tasks. Rawson writes about Alfred, a ten year old, who summarises the difficulty: *"I can think OK. What's wrong is just my words. I forget them and I can't manage them"*. (Critchley, 1970).

Literature dealing with dyslexia is uniform in its suggestion that dyslexia is an intrinsic developmental anomaly, the cause and expression of which is qualitatively different from reading difficulties arising from environmental factors. Dr. Margaret Snowling (1987) comments on the developmental nature of the disorder: *"its nature can be expected to change according to the age of the individual tested and the stage of development they have reached"*.

Maturation Lag

The developmental perspective is primarily a way of looking at individuals who appear to have language processing problems from birth and therefore display a 'maturation lag' in their progress in school, especially in reading and spelling. A common way of determining which children are dyslexic is to identify those who are more than two years behind the norm in reading and spelling for their chronological age and IQ, and who have normal neurological, psychiatric and social histories.

This section gives a brief overview of some research which has identified certain crucial pre-requisites which are needed for the acquisition of complex language skills involved in reading and writing. If there is an underdevelopment in maturation (which may be due to a mild neurological dysfunction), then diagnosis and identification of the dysfunction can be a basis for introducing a programme of individualised teaching which, if applied early enough, will succeed in helping the child catch up with their peer group, minimise the difficulty in later years and help develop their true potential.

Various studies have examined language development in children in an attempt to identify predictors of reading failure. Jansky and de Hirsch (1972) reported that picture naming was a good predictor of reading failure. This failure to name pictures had little to do with spatiality as many dyslexic children have well developed spatial skills (Newton, 1974) but was more a function of late or faulty language development.

Satz (1978) suggests that reading failure stems from a lag in maturation of the brain which delays those skills that are in primary ascendancy at different chronological ages. The skills that develop early (visual-motor and cross-modal sensory integration) are more likely to be delayed in younger children who are developmentally immature. Skills which develop later (language and formal operations) are more likely to be delayed in older children who are immature. His theory predicts that pre-school children who do not develop the primary perception skills will fail to acquire reading proficiency. Even if they should catch up on this particular maturation lag, they will have further difficulties due to their language processing problems.

Phonological Awareness

Bradley and Bryant (1985) examined whether it was possible to intervene and remediate at an early age children who were behind in reading. In their studies, they found that a normal part of the linguistic development of a child involved the construction of words and rhymes in word play. This play occurred even before the child started school and although the activity was unconscious, the child was already learning to analyse syllabic units and phonemic correlations. Their studies showed that ability to rhyme is one of the most significant indicators of later success in learning to read.

Children need to develop such meta-linguistic skills to deconstruct the printed word at a later date. Many dyslexic children are insensitive to such phonological connections and treat each word as if it is unique; they therefore have no schema for organising and generalising which make reading manageable for a child. Various studies have shown that children who do not have such meta-linguistic skills are not able to make the same progress in reading and writing as others in their peer group.

Bryant and Bradley's research identified indicators of the late development of reading skills and set up a studies to see if and what sort of intervention could help. In one study, groups of six year old children were given systematic training in categorising sounds through using rhyming groups and picture cards. In the second year children from one of the groups were also taught, using plastic letters, to make connections between sounds and letter patterns. When tested, the children using both sounds and letters showed marked improvement in reading. Children in control groups receiving no training or training in semantic categorisation did not show such improvement. Children who were taught only to categorise sounds also showed improvement, but not as much as those taught sounds and letters together.

Other studies showed that children who did not receive any special training in phonemic and alphabetic awareness at the age of six but received such help at the age of eight showed improvement also, but this was not as significant as with the younger age group.

These studies suggest that early intervention can alleviate some symptoms of developmental dyslexia and prevent pupils from lagging behind in spelling, reading and writing. Later intervention is less effective and such pupils will continue to show classic symptoms of dyslexia. This suggests that the developmental stage at which intervention is made may be crucial; and to quote Lynette Bradley, "We need to intervene as early as possible . . . Clearly, the policy of allocating resources *after failure has occurred* needs changing." [our italics]

Stages in Learning to Read

Uta Frith developed a developmental model of reading which identifies three main phases when learning to read. First, there is a **logographic** phase, whereby words are recognised by visual features, eg two sticks in 'umbrella'; second, an **alphabetic** or word building phase, based on phonemic blending and analysis; and third, an **orthographic** stage which is based on word recognition using visual and lexical analysis independent of sound, or at least where sound is integrated into word structure. The efficient reader relies on this orthographic stage of rapid word recognition.

If a child gets 'stuck' at the first, second or third stage, then she will not become a competent reader. Frith's model is a useful way of looking at reading problems in the light of the particular stage of reading at which the child may be 'stuck'. At the logographic stage, "letter order is largely ignored and phonological factors are entirely secondary" (Frith, 1980). At this stage, a child with visual perceptual problems may perceive a scrambled version of the real word or have difficulty discriminating or remembering visual features.

In the alphabetic stage children try to work words out using a grapheme to phoneme (letter-sound) conversion strategy. At this stage, even with an ability to use phonics, children with a visual processing difficulty could experience difficulties as they may translate a sequence of letters they perceive incorrectly as a non-word.

Theoretical Perspectives

Alternatively, children with phonological processing difficulties will not be able to put the sound to the symbol and cannot master this second stage. Such children might eventually 'jump' to the third stage but will be unable to fully use the alphabetic system to generalise from known to unknown words.

The third stage of Frith's model, the orthographic, relies on rapid word recognition. It occurs when children have acquired a store of learned words or internalised lexicon, and can therefore quickly retrieve this vocabulary when reading. Readers with visual processing difficulties may be stuck at the alphabetic stage and have difficulties with recognising or re-visualising words in order to have easy access to the internal lexicon.

A developmental perspective therefore may shed light on the various ways in which the course of language acquisition may fail to run smoothly. It also shows that developmental language disorders do not form a single entity but may affect different aspects of processing written language.

For those involved in teaching and supporting young people and adults with written language difficulties, a developmental perspective is useful to highlight the stage of development at which a student ceased to make progress in written language. Such information may help the tutor to form a tentative hypothesis which can be further tested or validated from observation of reading and spelling.

However, it must be stressed that teaching strategies which follow on from the maturational development, capacities, needs and, above all, interests of children are very often inappropriate for adults. Bradley's research is an interesting example how strategies used with very young children were not as successful when applied to an older age group.

Adults find many strategies adapted from primary teaching methods not only childish but ineffective. Adults have well established neurological pathways for processing perceptual and linguistic information, as well as fully and often highly developed cognitive processes which they may utilise to compensate for linguistic processing weaknesses. Dyslexic adults have established cognitive patterns which frequently reflect global and holistic ways of learning. They are therefore less likely to respond to phonological training but rather to compensate with visual and/or semantic strategies based on concrete personal experience. It is more effective to help them explore and come to understand their perceptual strengths and weaknesses and develop personal strategies based on their perceptual and lexical strengths, rather than trying to remediate a faulty perceptual processing system.

IV How Can I Help?

Supporting dyslexic students in further and higher education

Learning support needs to be seen as the responsibility of the whole institution if it is to be successful. In addition to specialist learning support, students will need support from subject staff and may also need technological aids, extended loan periods for library books and other resources, careers advice which takes into account their particular strengths and difficulties, technical help to learn to use specialist equipment, counselling to help them come to terms with their disability and admissions staff who can give appropriate advice and guidance about courses.

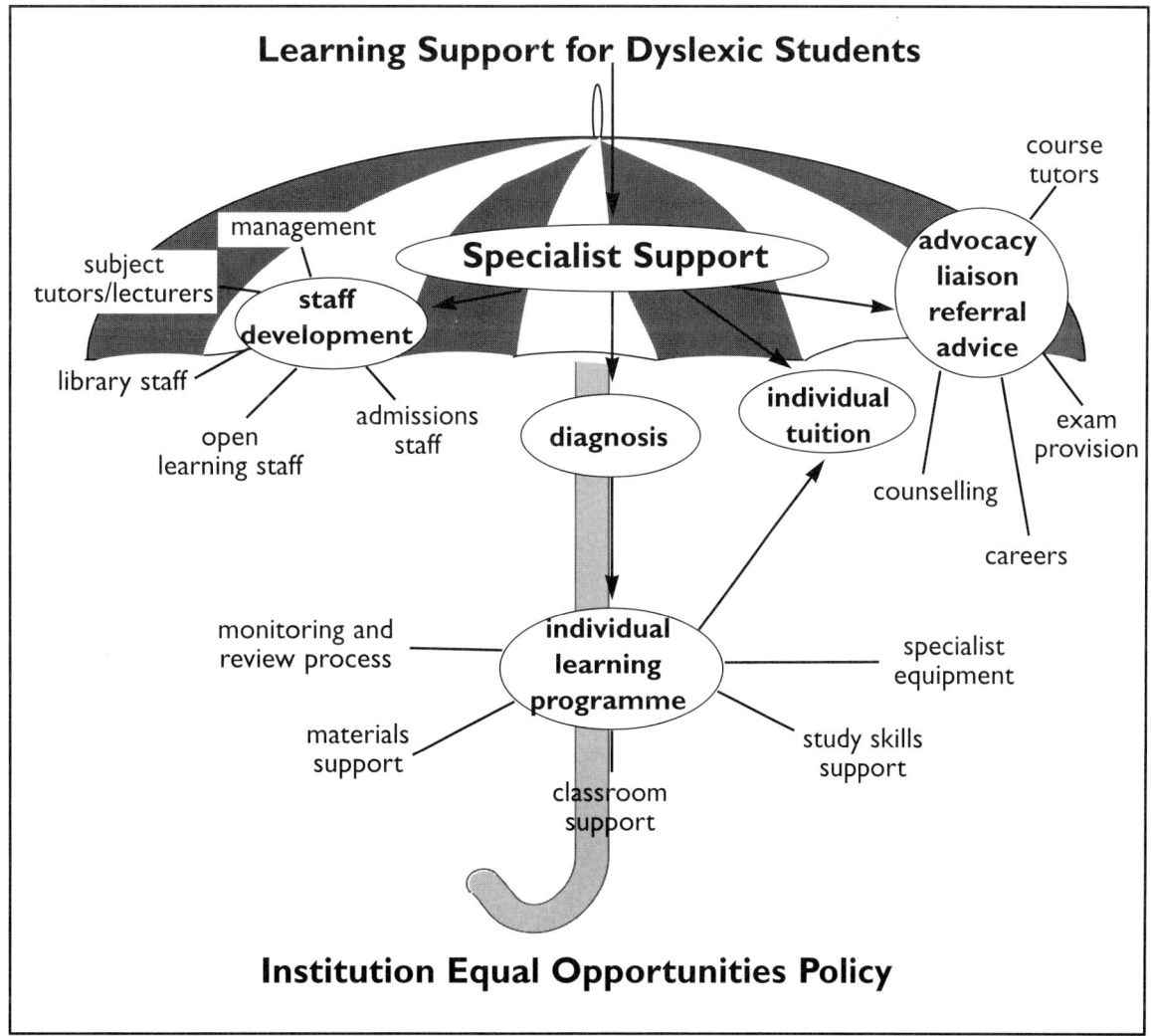

How Can I Help?

Learning support model

A model for meeting dyslexic students' support needs should include effective systems for:

- referral
- diagnostic assessment and feed-back
- identifying the various types of support the student needs
- designing a learning programme for additional learning support
- delivery of support within the total learning environment

To be truly responsive, a support structure would have:

- *a trained co-ordinator* responsible for ensuring delivery of support throughout the institution and co-ordinating a network of trained learning support staff.
- *a cross-institution network of staff* who can support students within the total learning environment.

Dyslexia should also be included as a *named disability* in Equal Opportunities and Language Policies. It is important to include it in any language policy because it is primarily a disability which manifests itself in students' written language.

A clear system for accessing resources is also necessary to ensure that students receive appropriate support and that available funding is used to maximum effect.

Dyslexic students are included among those eligible for additional support through FEFC funding. This additional funding has been given in recognition that without specific, directed support, students with learning difficulties and disabilities, of which dyslexia is one, will not achieve successful learning outcomes. The consequence of this additional funding is that colleges need to evolve a strategic plan to implement effective and quick identification of need and delivery of the service; as without a system in place, colleges will not only fail students but also risk losing funding revenue.

In higher education, full time students are eligible for the Disabled Students Allowance which must be applied for from their local education authority. The allowance covers additional costs incurred by the disability such as extra photocopying and the purchase of a computer. Part of the allowance may be used for specific specialist help or to pay for an amanuensis or a reader. In order to qualify for this allowance, a diagnosis of dyslexia is necessary.

Dyslexia support

An additional support plan should address the range and network of support required and any aids to learning that the student will need.

a. **Initial diagnosis and follow-up**

   Time will need to be allowed for *diagnostic procedures* which involve the following:

   - the diagnostic assessment (at least one and half hours)
   - writing a report (at least one hour)
   - discussing the report, counselling the student and drawing up a learning plan (at least one hour)
   - liaison with course tutors and other support staff (this should be recognised as an integral function of support)

b. **Specialist tuition and support**

   After the initial diagnostic assessment, hours are needed to enable *one-to-one tuition*. This is necessary for at least a short period and should be conducted by appropriately trained staff. It is important that staff are trained to teach adults as well as dyslexic learners.

   Sometimes, small group support with other dyslexic students is possible after students have begun to understand their difficulties, appreciate their learning style, be aware of their learning strengths and weaknesses and develop successful learning strategies.

c. **Liaison and staff development with subject staff and development or adaptation of materials**

   In some cases the specialist staff may work with subject staff to adapt materials, introduce learning and teaching strategies and explore ways of improving students' access to the curriculum. Subject lecturers and course tutors need to be active participants in supporting learning.

d. **On site facilities including a private room.**

   An identified room, appropriately resourced and easily accessible to students, needs to be available for diagnosis and individual tuition. This is essential for the confidential and often emotional nature of the diagnostic interview, but also for teaching since many dyslexic students are distracted by a noisy environment.

e. **Examination provision**

   Specialist examination provision for dyslexic students is an important part of additional support and should be arranged early in the course. Requests should be related to students' specific needs and to the particular examination.

Examples of the kind of provision which can be made according to the individual's difficulties and which should be specified in the diagnostic report include:

- extra time (the amount is negotiable)
- a reader to read the exam questions
- an amanuensis to write down dictated responses to the questions
- the use of a word-processor (in GCSE examinations, a spell check is not allowed)
- an extra invigilator if a private room is needed

In-house diagnostic reports by trained dyslexia support staff are usually acceptable for receiving special provision. However, GCSE and A Level Boards require that these reports be underwritten by an educational psychologist. There is normally a fee for this service. In some cases psychologists may need to see the student.

f. Technological aids

Various equipment should be made available specifically for the use of dyslexic students. Items which are invaluable for supporting learning and achieving success are:

- hand held spell-checks such as the Franklin Spellmaster
- personal computers with a spell-check and thesaurus
- computer software packages such as 'Thinksheet'
- Walkmans or tape recorders to use as a memory aid, to record notes and lectures, and to listen to reading materials

(For further information see section on learning aids and equipment)

g. Student Support Groups

The underlying purpose of dyslexia support is to foster individual autonomy and to develop self confidence and successful compensating strategies. Student support groups enable dyslexic students to meet and discuss their difficulties and problems with one another and offer opportunities for students to share strategies for overcoming obstacles to success. Often these are initiated by students themselves. It is usually helpful if meetings are initially organised by the dyslexia support co-ordinator, who, after a few meetings, becomes a facilitator and scribe to note suggestions, further the group's development or take up issues of concern on students' behalf.

h.   Advocacy

The difficulties which dyslexic students experience in education are many and varied. They are often embarrassed to raise issues with their course tutor or subject lecturer and often rely on their dyslexia support tutor to raise such matters with the teacher concerned on their behalf. Advocacy is often necessary in cases of access and progression to courses, examination and assignment provision, the provision of technological aids or to ensure that the dyslexic student is not treated in an unfair manner within the classroom.

Specialist diagnosis and tuition

Dyslexia is a complex and subtle disability which often looks like carelessness, lack of attention, or incompetence and nearly all dyslexic students will have suffered negative labels and misunderstanding.

They will therefore need help to:

- understand the nature of their disability and how it affects their learning and their lives

- work through any anger that follows the initial relief at having a name for their difficulties and any bitterness about lack of support during their previous learning experiences

A diagnostic assessment is needed to identify the nature of the student's difficulties and how these may affect course work and assessment, in order to advise on the most appropriate course and to plan a programme of support to meet that individual's needs.

Many students returning to education have failed at school because their difficulties were never identified or appropriately addressed. For them, receiving a diagnosis of dyslexia is to have their difficulties acknowledged for the first time in their lives. The diagnostic process should be one which helps them understand their difficulties and assures them of their ability to learn and to succeed.

A written diagnostic report based on the assessment should fulfil all or some of the following purposes:

- *form a framework* on which to counsel and advise students on the disability and to work through past failure

- *clarify the nature of the difficulties* for students and relevant others

- *suggest an effective learning programme* for additional support, based on an analysis of individual strengths and weaknesses

- *inform* subject staff on appropriate and relevant teaching methods and strategies for supporting students within the course context

How Can I Help?

- *provide evidence* of students additional learning needs for FEFC funding or the Disabled Students Allowance

- *make recommendations for examining boards* when students need to seek special provision

Dyslexic learners learn best with a structured, individualised programme geared to their particular strengths and weaknesses. They also learn best in a highly meaningful context, based on their own writing and personal associations. General study skills approaches and worksheets commonly used in basic skills workshops and open learning centres are rarely useful as dyslexic students have difficulties generalising and transferring 'abstract' learning.

Specialist tuition is therefore necessary for at least an initial period; it should be based on the diagnostic assessment and aim to:

- *confirm* students' intelligence and basic ability to learn

- *'unpack'* the difficulties so that students can begin to identify their own strengths and weaknesses and preferred learning style

- *explore*, identify and help them find strategies which will work for them individually, based on their cognitive strengths

- *unlearn* 'bad habits' or the use of inappropriate strategies

- *set up and implement* an individualised programme of structured learning related to their course

- *help* students to practice appropriate and effective methods of study

- *monitor* the success of methods and strategies as part of encouraging students to take control of their own learning

- *make* the learning process *explicit*

- *give them space for self-discovery and experience of success*

Staff development: raising awareness

If dyslexic students are to receive adequate and appropriate support, ***all staff*** need to be alert to behaviour or problems which may indicate dyslexic difficulties and to be aware of referral procedures and support needs.

When dyslexia is not identified, lecturers may be impatient with students who persistently misspell easy words, miscopy from the board, misunderstand what they say or are unable to keep up with other students. Careers advisers may suggest inappropriate courses or guidance counsellors may assume a student cannot follow a certain course of study because of poor literacy skills.

When staff come to understand both the nature of the difficulties and the different learning style of dyslexic students, they can address students' needs in a more sympathetic and constructive way.

Guidelines for tutors and lecturers

It is not unusual for subject teachers to panic when they are faced with having to teach a dyslexic student in their class. They sometimes feel they do not have the expertise, suitable strategies or time to meet the learning needs of such students.

Some dyslexic students may present a challenge to even the most experienced teacher. However, our experience has shown that many teachers through understanding and ingenuity have evolved a range of teaching methods, strategies and assessment procedures which have enabled dyslexic students to succeed and gain confidence and autonomy as learners.

The following suggestions may not suit every dyslexic student, nor all teachers, but they have all worked with a great number of students within a variety of contexts.

General overview

- Remember that dyslexic students are often intelligent and creative. Their disability means that they process language based tasks more slowly and in a more convoluted way than non-dyslexic students. This does not mean they cannot eventually succeed at a task; it will simply take them longer.

- Many teachers rely on language to get their points across. Dyslexic students often have a 'right brain' dominance - this means that they respond better to visual or other modes of representation. Albert Einstein, who was dyslexic, found language based tasks irrelevant to his way of thinking:

"The words of the language, as they are written or spoken, do not seem to play any role in my mechanism of thought."
(Quoted in West, 1991)

- Find out how they learn. Examine your own assumptions about learning.

- Begin by observing and listening to dyslexic students and use them as a resource. Then try and implement what they tell you - they often know what they need!

It may seem impractical or unnecessary to change your teaching for the sake of one or two students. However, many of the approaches which help dyslexic students will help all students learn more effectively.

How Can I Help?

Holistic and 'right brain' approaches to teaching

- Adapt your teaching methods to meet the learning style of the dyslexic student. For instance, many dyslexics are 'holistic' thinkers; they may be able to grasp complex interrelationships at once but they often do not respond to step by step instruction.

- Help students to understand their own preferred learning style and find strategies which utilise their learning strengths.

- Give an overview of the topic and provide a framework by stating the aims of the class and the expected outcome. Once students have an overall idea what to expect, they can more easily make sense of the step by step logic of the lesson.

- Use a variety of audio-visual methods including videos, tapes, pictures, demonstrations and diagrams. Utilise the dyslexic student's ability to 'think in pictures'.

- Set up experiential and 'hands-on' activities which allow students to bring existing skills to the present task.

Addressing the student's learning needs

- Recognise that dyslexia is a difficulty with the automatic processing of language. Therefore explicitly introduce new words/terms or concepts. Give plenty of examples for the new vocabulary/terminology to become meaningful and give students opportunities to practise the vocabulary and to recognise it in print.

- Don't rely on talking alone to deliver your subject matter - vary the pace and activities used in the session. For example, set up structured discussions and presentations in small groups which give students opportunities to experiment with language while discussing ideas and opinions - and to use their motor memory!

- When lecturing, give the framework, overview and main points at the beginning and give 'markers' along the way to help students distinguish important points.

- Allow time for students to process information - break lectures into chunks with pauses for taking it in and time for questions. Break up learning tasks into small steps and allow time for reinforcement and 'over-learning' of information.

- Encourage students to formulate questions, then respond using straightforward language and demonstrate your points with concrete examples.

- Build in lots of feedback to monitor student's understanding and develop their learning skills.

- Some dyslexic students may need to sit at the back of the room so as not to be distracted by people sitting behind them. Allow them to sit where they hear best.

- Many dyslexic students get lost in following sequences and following instructions, so may need help in action planning and prioritising tasks.

- Perhaps the most important advice is to be pragmatic and eclectic. If one method does not work, try another - until the student feels comfortable with the methods or strategies used.

Note-taking

As dyslexic students may have difficulties with spelling, writing quickly and copying, note-taking is particularly stressful for them.

- If you dictate notes, consider alternative approaches such as giving out skeleton notes, simplified copies of your own notes, setting up directed reading activities with discussion, introducing mind-maps or allowing the use of tape-recorders.

- If using an overhead projector, type the information using a readable size of print. Limit the amount of information on each overhead transparency to key points. Elaboration of key points should be given to the group on a separate handout. In this way the students have access to information which they may miss during the lesson and can read at home at their own pace.

- Use black/white boards **only** to give examples, elaborate a point or note key words or concepts or names - **never** for extensive note-taking. Make sure your writing is large and clear and students can read it.

- Allow the use of tape-recorders or lap top computers in lectures, if the student feels this is necessary.

Production of materials

All students deserve handouts which are of a high quality both in layout and content. It is especially so in the case of dyslexic students who often get discouraged by not having the same access to information as other students due to their difficulties in processing language.

- Where helpful, use coloured paper for photocopies. The preferred colour varies - so experiment with different backgrounds. (Blue is the most commonly preferred).

- Use a larger print type font which is clear if producing materials yourself. Be aware that some type faces are more difficult to read than others - this varies with the student.

How Can I Help?

- Use line settings which are not crowded. The space between words should always be clear so letters do not seem jumbled together.

- Enlarge copies if photocopying. **Never** reduce the size of print!

- Wherever possible use plenty of diagrams, mind-maps or pictures.

- Do not present too much information on one sheet.

- Do not justify right-hand margins. This makes the space between the words uneven and makes it difficult for dyslexic students to follow the print.

- Make sure the lines of print are not too long. An average of 12 words to a line is normal. Make type bigger and margins wider if information is complex. This makes 'tracking' of print easier for the dyslexic student.

Assignments/examinations

- Give specific instructions for assignments/essays. Explain essay titles or the purpose of the assignment explicitly as dyslexic students can easily misunderstand the question. Check students' understanding and don't give out assignments in a rush at the last minute.

- Avoid unnecessarily complex language when writing assignment or exam questions. Also avoid long and syntactically complex sentences.

- Some dyslexic students are intuitive thinkers - they grasp concepts very quickly. What they cannot do well is to transfer their ideas onto paper! Their ideas get muddled and this affects sentence structure and essay organisation. Encourage dyslexic students to get additional support to develop writing techniques.

- Allow an extended period for assignment writing. Help the student break down the assignment into chunks or 'steps' so it is manageable.

- Allow assignment work to be word-processed and ensure the student learns how to use the word processor.

- When marking students' work, try and separate your marking of transcription errors (spelling, punctuation, written expression, vocabulary) and of content, so that the student's knowledge and understanding is acknowledged and valued.

- Try to be aware that dyslexic students have to rewrite work many times over before they hand it in and that they may proofread their work several times and still never see their errors. ***Never accuse a dyslexic student of being careless or lazy - they often work twice as hard.***

Special exam provision

The following kinds of special provision may be appropriate depending on the individual student's difficulties:

- **Extra time** can be given to the student for the reading of the exam questions and for writing and checking their work. This allowance varies with individual examination boards and the needs of the student.

- **Consideration** for spelling, written expression and organisational difficulty are appropriate for most dyslexic students.

- **A reader** may be requested to read the exam questions to the student. This is useful if the questions are long and complex or the student is likely to misread the questions.

- **An amanuensis or scribe** writes down the answers which are dictated by the student. A scribe is usually requested when there is evidence of severe handwriting or expressive difficulties.

- A **word-processor** should be requested when students have considerable writing difficulties and are used to word-processing their work.

- A **'viva voce'** or oral examination may be appropriate where students have great difficulty with the written word.

Show understanding

The problems of dyslexia can be extremely frustrating for students. Try and be supportive if students say they are dyslexic - don't think this is an excuse. Ask them how you as a teacher can help.

Setting up a learning programme

To be successful, a learning programme for dyslexic young people and adults should be based on the following principles:

- that diagnostic assessment is essential in helping students to understand previous learning failure, 'unpack' the disability, identify strengths and well as weaknesses and thus shift self-perceptions and expose learning 'myths'

- that approaches to teaching and support should be 'diagnostic' in helping students explore and identify personal learning strategies which suit their individual learning style, and thus encourage autonomy in learning

- that support is an **enabling** rather than remedial process, which should be seen as a way of matching the total learning environment to the learner's individual needs and goals and so involving in its delivery **all** staff with whom the student is in contact

Diagnostic assessment

The diagnostic process will need to be carried out by an appropriately trained tutor. A recommended methodology would consist of:

- a preliminary in depth interview with the student to determine the learning history and pattern of difficulties and strengths

- an analysis of reading miscues and reading style together with an oral comprehension

- a spelling error analysis based on a diagnostic dictation

- an analysis of the student's own free writing

- a written report summarising the student's processing difficulties with recommendations for teaching strategies to employ both in individual support sessions and in the classroom, and for any special examination provision

- a feedback session to talk through the diagnosis with the student so that it can be used as a springboard for future learning.

Only after a full diagnosis is made can a suitable programme be drawn up to meet the specific learning needs of that particular student. The diagnosis therefore provides a framework for the development of effective learning.

[For details of an appropriate diagnostic process for young people and adults, see *Klein, C, Diagnosing Dyslexia.*]

Planning for success

Any learning programme must enable the student to succeed. Many dyslexic students have underachieved in the past through inappropriate teaching methods and now regard themselves as failures. An important function of learning support is to help students understand that any previous academic failure was not their fault and to show them that through the use of an individualised programme based on strategies which reflect their own learning strengths, they can and will make progress.

There are three essential criteria for a successful learning programme:

- it needs to be relevant and specific to the student's individual learning needs, goals and context

- it should provide an immediate experience of success

- it should enable students to become active learners through understanding the way they learn and so eventually to take charge of their own learning.

As the learning programme begins, a careful framework has to be established so that the student has a secure understanding of the learning process. The learning experience needs to be an active interaction between the tutor and learner, with both parties reflecting upon whether a particular strategy has been successful or not. This means giving the student space to explore and clarify with the tutor issues concerned with the learning process.

Learning how to learn

Perhaps the saddest experience which dyslexic students bring to support sessions is one of continued failure and low self esteem. While at school, lists of spellings were usually given out for students to learn; in most cases however, no strategies were given for learning the words, nor was any interest shown in *why* some students failed to learn these words while others in their peer group did. They therefore were made to feel it was their fault, through laziness or stupidity, that they were bad spellers. Their failure to learn spellings merely reinforced their negative self image of themselves as learners. Finding out why they experienced these problems enables learners to gain self-esteem and feel confident to proceed with *learning how they learn.*

Many students are hampered in their attempts to make progress due to old remembered myths, namely "if you read more your spelling will improve", or "I can't spell because I don't pronounce words right". In order to help students unlearn such misconceptions, tutors should share their knowledge of language and the learning and spelling processes to empower students as learners. Part of the process of building confidence entails an assurance that they will not continue to be given "more of the same" methods which failed repeatedly in the past.

Other students are afraid to put pen to paper due to unpleasant and demeaning experiences with spelling and writing at school. They need to understand that they do not need to be good spellers before they are allowed to write the words they want to use; but that 'inventing' their own spellings can show what they do and do not know about spelling and what they need to learn, as well as freeing them to express their ideas more satisfactorily.

Unlearning is part of the process of learning. Students need to know why methods or strategies suggested in the past have not worked for them and to analyse why they continue to make certain types of errors and not others.

They also need to know how successful learners learn, how competent writers write and how good spellers spell. For instance, many students are surprised that good spellers do not 'sound-out' words, nor do they call out individual letters as they write them.

They are also surprised to learn that good spellers often feel their hand when they make a mistake in writing a word and automatically stop, look at the word and then see where the mistake has been made; that is they are using visual-motor skills.

Implementing a Learning Programme

An effective learning programme will develop students' awareness of their processing strengths and weaknesses.

It should be organised around each student's preferred learning style, using strategies based on strengths to compensate for weaknesses.

It should also develop transferable learning skills. Students need to be able to internalize learning within the context of their actual assignments. The use of exercise sheets or rules are nearly always ineffective because dyslexic students do not spontaneously generalise learning or transfer it to other contexts. Instead, support should be related to identified difficulties which the student is having with current assignments or projects, so that the student can observe, learn, practice and adopt the skills they need for each particular piece of work and gradually transfer these skills to other situations.

A key factor in success that student and tutor *reflect* together on the success or failure of attempted strategies. It is particularly valuable in cases where something has been effective that the reasons for that success be made *explicit.*

Discussion of learning needs to be an essential part of every support session so that students discover strategies that work best for them and practise and reflect on these. Tutors will need to carefully observe learning and facilitate both understanding and application through reinforcement and overlearning. They need to *listen* to students as well, and support their growing autonomy as learners.

Developing effective strategies

Both tutor and student must be actively involved in exploring and evaluating strategies for learning . They must also prioritise learning needs since dyslexic people sometimes seem to have so many problems that both student and tutor may be overwhelmed. These needs should be regularly updated to meet the demands of the course. The importance of reading and writing regularly must be constantly stressed, as without revision and practice, little progress will be made.

Spelling is often a student's most immediate learning need and an individualised spelling programme can be a good starting point for helping students identify their learning strengths and weaknesses and establish transferable learning skills.

A spelling programme appears to be very time consuming at the beginning stages but it provides an opportunity for students to experience concrete measurable success and begin to understand their own learning. Strategies for learning each selected word should be based on observation and analysis of the student's actual spelling attempts and include discussion with students about what they know about spelling as well as what they do not. To be effective, strategies must 'fit' and be **owned** by students.

Words to be learned should be selected from students' own writing and be words they use and want to learn.

Once a word is chosen by the students, the tutor discusses the reasons why the student spelt the word in that particular way. For instance if *'psychology'* is spelt as *'sicology'*, does the student know why she spelled it that way? Does she find it difficult to remember how it looks? Does she know the root of the word or what it means? It is through such discussions that students become aware of their particular learning style and processing strengths and weaknesses.

Learning the selected spellings involves practising them according to the chosen strategies for remembering. It also involves checking back to identify any errors. This process of self-checking is the basis of the acquisition of transferable learning skills.

[For a full discussion of setting up and implementing an individualised spelling programme, see Klein and Millar 1991 and Klein 1991]

It is very important to break the pattern of learning failure so strategies used should be individualised according to the student's processing strengths and learning style. For instance, it is not helpful to ask a student with auditory processing difficulties to listen to how a word sounds.

Students with visual processing difficulties will often be able to 'sound out' syllables or chunks. Their mistakes often take the form of good phonic alternatives but lack the 'look' of the word, eg *'parculear '* for *'peculiar'*.

How Can I Help?

The learning approach in this case would perhaps entail:

- explaining how the student is spelling (explaining the logic she is adopting when using the phonic alternative)
- why she has adopted phonic strategies
- why the word is not spelt phonetically (ie examining the nature of the English spelling system)
- examining the roots of the word, prefixes, suffixes, (if appropriate)
- making up a spelling pronunciation, exaggerating the sound of **p** and **li** (as in 'lie'): **pe**(e) **cu**(e) **li**(e) **ar**(e)
- making up a mnemonic, eg "**p** eter's **ecu** is a **li**ar"
- tapping out syllables or parts of words to help tracking
- experimenting with highlighters to reinforce visual patterns within the word - especially helpful in cases of visual-motor tracking difficulties.
- explaining the importance of motor memory for spelling and the need for joined-up handwriting

Students with auditory processing difficulties may write words which bear little resemblance to the orthodox spelling due to sounds being misheard, mis-sequenced or omitted. An example of such a spelling would be writing 'satefasion' for 'satisfaction'. Such students often have good sight vocabularies and tend to learn the look of words in order to write them. Their visual strengths should be utilised and encouraged and a suitable learning programme may include the following:

- explaining how the student is spelling (eg reasons why he cannot discriminate sounds or hold the sounds of parts of words in the auditory memory for long enough to write the word)
- explaining why adopting a 'sounding-out' method does not work
- explaining his visual perceptual strengths and how they can be used as a basis for the creation of spelling strategies
- finding words within words, eg **sat is fact ion**
- using highlighters to give visual emphasis to parts of words which tend to be misheard or are missed out: **is fact**
- using personal mnemonics to remember the difficult sounds
- learning to find lexical patterns which can be linked with other similar words - a good starting point may be studies of prefixes, suffixes and common letter patterns.
- finding visually striking patterns in words, eg **r ece ive** or chunking into visually and lexically memorable units, eg **br ill i ant**

The kinaesthetic sense can be reinforced by encouraging the use of joined-up handwriting, especially when practising spellings as part of a spelling programme. Students may find that using a fountain pen which drags more on the paper reinforces motor-memory and helps control. It is useful to experiment with pens at the beginning of a spelling programme. Some students may find tracing letters useful. In cases where problems are severe, sand-paper letters can be used for feeling the shape of the letter to help the motor memory.

A tutor knows when students are becoming autonomous learners when they tell the tutor:

"*No, that won't work for me, because* … "

"*I think we should do it this way because* …."

For some students, even a short period working in this way can change their entire view of themselves as learners.

Developing Language Skills

Success in a spelling programme creates the self confidence students need to develop and experiment with writing. They soon realise that the learning skills developed through self analysis and evaluation can be transferred to other areas of study.

Writing

Dyslexic students need support in all areas of language use and often need to have issues of language made explicit. Writing skills often present dyslexic students with many difficulties as students often complain that they know what they want to write but can't get it down on paper. Support should be based on the student's own writing and focus on developing the following:

- an understanding of metacognitive and metalinguistic skills - thinking about thinking and talking about language.

- awareness of how to use the conventions and schemas of formal writing through exploring 'models' - what is an 'introduction'? a paragraph? a 'reference"?

- planning of essays using 'mind maps', (see Buzan 1982), or spider diagrams - dyslexic students find it difficult to put ideas into sequences so it is useful to find non-linear ways to help them put ideas together. Highlighters can be used to colour code ideas which should be grouped together, and putting all the groupings in order can be done last.

- organisation of writing - students need a structure to develop, expand and order their writing. Often many ideas get confused into one sentence or paragraph; disentangling such writing is possible by the use of working on topic and 'kernel' sentences (see Shaughnessy 1977), dictating onto a tape or having the tutor scribe so the student does not have to write and think simultaneously.

- specific examples of 'genres' and formats to explain aspects of style, tone, register and structures suitable for different writing purposes.

- self correcting or proofreading skills - these can be linked to a spelling programme and developed through error analysis marking; that is, indicating the type of error in the margin for students to find and correct themselves. This can be used as the beginning of a dialogue to discover students' confusions about what is expected of them.

Reading

Observation of a student's reading style and difficulties should inform the choice of appropriate reading strategies. For instance, students with visual processing difficulties often experience difficulties with word recognition and even if they seem to be competent readers, continue to experience problems with comprehension.

In such instances, the tutor can encourage the development of comprehension skills through helping the student become aware of the reading process and teaching the student to evolve techniques of previewing, questioning what they have read, monitoring their comprehension, and reflecting on the passage in question.

Tutors need to be aware that some students with visual processing difficulties experience visual disturbances of print, making reading extremely stressful and tiring. The use of coloured acetate overlays or masking cards to keep their place may help, as may soft lighting and different fonts and print sizes.

Students with auditory processing difficulties will have difficulty deciphering new words in print or distinguishing between similar looking words out of context. New words need to be discussed and learned preparatory to reading a text. Working on spelling often helps these students to develop visual and lexical ways into words which can help build their sight vocabulary.

Dyslexic students will also need to help to select texts which are well structured and accessible as well as to find alternative ways to get information, such as videos and television programmes.

Study Skills

A learning programme will also include support for other difficulties which dyslexic students may have. For instance, dyslexic students often have problems with organising themselves and their work. In some cases, the disorganisation is so great that the tutor not only has to discuss reasons why folders need to be neat and assignments easily found, but also show students how and where to place items behind the appropriate dividers. Weekly checking ensures that students are keeping to the agreed filing system and are encouraged to extend their 'repertoire' of organisational strategies by using year planners, diaries, and colour coding.

One dyslexic student developed his own coded system for planning his studies and organising his notes, devised learning and revision strategies based around coloured highlighters to help keep him 'on course' and eventually became the most organised student in his group!

Students will also need to learn and practise strategies for note-taking and studying for exams. They may also need help with planning their assignments.

Students must experience success; otherwise they will get disheartened and their sense of failure will return. The learning programme should be negotiated at the beginning, with small achievable chunks of success. For some students this may mean only learning six or eight words a week at the beginning - but this will still constitute 100% success; in many cases, more than a student has ever achieved before.

There is no 'magic wand' to make learning difficulties disappear, but students soon realise that with a regular, systematic approach they can and do make considerable progress.

In addition to developing strategies to compensate for weaknesses, it is important to help students discover and value their particular non-linguistic strengths. They may be able to see interrelationships between ideas more quickly and accurately and may be able to generate creative solutions to problems through using visual-spatial approaches or an intuitive understanding of how systems work. These gifts also need to be explored as resources for learning and as a source of confidence in meeting difficulties and contributing to the learning process.

Technological and learning aids

There are a number of technological and learning aids which can make an enormous difference to the success of dyslexic students. The following aids have been found to be helpful:

File dividers and organisers

As dyslexic students tend to be very messy and disorganised, organisation aids can help them overcome some of the stress which studying will place upon them. Colour coding helps organisation, as does using labels and plastic wallets to help identify separate pieces of work.

Franklin Spellmasters

These are hand-held spell-checks which can be easily carried and used unobtrusively when having to produce written work. They also have functions for distinguishing homonyms and some models include a thesaurus.

Micro-cassette or mini-tape recorder

These are easy to carry, and very useful to record instructions or notes if the student cannot write them down to remember them. They can also be used to dictate essays or ideas which can later be written or to read texts onto tape and play back for improved comprehension.

Taped books

The tapes can be played when in a car or when listening to a Walkman. They can improve knowledge and vocabulary, help students access course content, revise or simply enable students to enjoy a good story. The tapes can also be part of a reading programme for beginner reader to encourage quicker reading and thus reading for pleasure.

Videos, films or television programmes

These should be made available and recommended wherever possible as resources for topics which students are studying. They give a meaningful context to the subject and give easy access to students with a 'global' learning style.

Electronic typewriter with spell-check

The Spellright electronic typewriter (Smith Corona) has a memory with a word processing programme and a dictionary with 75,000 words. When you type, it compares your spelling with the dictionary word and if you make a spelling mistake it will bleep and flash.

Kurzweil Personal Reader

This is a sophisticated and effective (if rather expensive) reading machine which translates typewritten materials such as letters, books and newspapers into speech which can be listened to through headphones or can be recorded onto cassettes. Although primarily for the visually disabled, dyslexic students could follow the sound track as an aid to comprehending text. The quality of the sound reproduction is excellent, with nine different tones of speech and speed available. The machine could provide instant access to pages of text books for students to study in the library.

A micro-computer

A word processing programme that includes a spell-check and thesaurus is invaluable in reducing handwriting, organisational, spelling and word-finding difficulties.

Soft-ware packages such as:

"Thinksheet". The screen starts off as a notepad, then helps the user develop ideas into a range of structures - study plans, essay plans etc. Ideas are put onto the screen in independent boxes and can contain a considerable amount of information. This information can be printed in box form or in a linear format. Each box acts as a 'door' to a secondary field so that the user never runs out of space in which to present ideas. Useful for those who have difficulty in getting their ideas down on paper. Available from Fischer Marriott, 3 Grove Road, Ansty, nr Coventry, Warwick CV7 9JD Tel: 01203-616325

"Mindmaps Plus". This is a mapping system that allows ideas to be organised around a central theme. There is also a colour coding facility to allow the linking of ideas. Available from: Cedar Software Ltd, Golf Course Road, Blairgowrie, Perthshire PH10 6LQ, Scotland Tel: 0250 875929

PAL (Predictive Adaptive Lexicon). This was developed for multi-handicapped students who have difficulty with speech or written work and find writing slow and frustrating. The user has a screen in front and a short menu of word predictions is shown. One of these may be selected (a new list comes up if not). The predictions are produced from a dictionary of words which contain statistical information relating to frequency and recency of use. Separate dictionaries can be set up for different topics. This can be useful for technical or ESOL students. The dictionary acquires the words you use. Available from Professor A Newall, Microcomputer Centre, University of Dundee, Dundee DD1 4HN.

"Monologue". This is a voice synthesiser which reads aloud text from a computer screen. It enables the user to hear any grammatical errors that might be missed when reading silently. It is also useful for students to hear

their ideas spoken aloud. Voice synthesisers help students with visual processing problems to proofread as it removes the visual discomfort experienced by some students when reading.

"Texthelp". This is a more sophisticated version of "Monologue" and is also available from: IANSYST Ltd, United House, North Road, London N7 9DP Tel: 0171 607 5844

IBM Speech Recognition System. This works by the user speaking into a microphone connected to the computer, which analyses the spoken words and turns them into text on the screen. The user has to 'train' the computer to recognise their speech patterns, but eventually users can dictate from 70 to 100 words a minute. Any correctly recognised word is automatically spelt accurately, so a spell-check is unnecessary. This package also has a sophisticated semantic store as it nearly always chooses correctly between homonyms such as 'to', 'too' and 'two' from the context in which they are used. Users can also listen back to hear what they have "written".

Employment, training and careers

*"The biggest problem about being dyslexic is other people - they come down hard on you when you make mistakes, and being dyslexic you make so **many** mistakes"*

There are many issues for the dyslexic person in training for employment and in getting and keeping a job:

- choosing a career or job which will maximise success
- selecting the right education or training route to qualifications
- filling in application forms and writing CVs
- dealing with the demands of the course or job
- finding compensating and enabling strategies
- other people's perceptions and assumptions

The more that careers and employment advisers or guidance counsellors know about dyslexia, the more helpful they can be in aiding dyslexic people to explore and identify the right job environment, career and course of study to fit their personal strengths and weaknesses.

Choosing a course or career: things to consider

The choice of a training course or career for dyslexic individuals should be based on their abilities and strengths, but with an awareness of their weaknesses. The latter is important because a key ingredient of success is finding effective ways to deal with areas of weakness.

What is important is not to assume that a dyslexic person's literacy skills should be addressed **before** pursuing a chosen course but to be aware that dyslexic people develop reading and writing skills best within a meaningful and content based context. Opportunities for alternative forms of assessment and special examination provision should also be considered. It is very disheartening to be denied access to what you are good at or what might develop you intellectually until you have improved your weak literacy skills.

Since many dyslexic people tend to think visually, spatially and holistically, they may have obvious talents in art, design, performing arts, engineering and science. Many top architects, scientists and engineers are dyslexic; they have a gift for visualising whole systems and how parts interact with one another.

These visual-spatial skills may, however, also be used to aid success in more traditionally academic areas. Dyslexic people have succeeded in every kind of field. Some jobs such as office and secretarial work specifically rely on the dyslexic person's greatest area of weakness (filing, organising, taking messages and typing accurately); these jobs should be avoided while remembering that dyslexic people may be excellent at business and will often succeed by developing personal strategies to compensate for their weaknesses. They will need to find an appropriate route or a job flexible enough to make use of their strengths without putting overwhelming demands on their weaknesses.

"Law is a great career for a dyslexic person - you can dictate everything for the secretary to type up"

Dyslexic individuals are also often good at hands-on and physical skills such as needed for building crafts, catering, computers, performing arts and sports. Although some have poor eye-hand coordination or are 'clumsy', others have been Olympic champions.

It is vital to remember that dyslexic people do not form a homogeneous group and that they have individual interests, talents and abilities like everyone else, as well as varying degrees of determination.

Which progression route?

Various aspects of a course or training route to qualifications will need to be taken into account: the general demands, the type of assessment, the way a course or training programme is delivered, the 'style' of teachers or trainers.

Some dyslexic individuals prefer a GNVQ or NVQ course involving continuous assessment; others find the pressure of continuous assessment too great because of the time needed to draft and redraft written assignments. Some find multiple choice tests very confusing because of difficulty recognising words out of context while others prefer them because they eliminate the need to write. Exam based GCSE and A levels may reduce some pressure on course work but put extensive demands on the memory and being able to write accurately at speed. It is important to consider what special examination provision is available as this varies for different types of courses, levels and validating bodies.

Dyslexic people may also have to accept that it may take them longer than others to achieve their goals - but they will still get there in the end!

What can employers do to help?

The most important thing employers, supervisers and colleagues can do is to understand what the dyslexic person's difficulties are and to appreciate that person's strengths.

Dyslexia can often look like incompetence. Understanding is vital in sorting out the one from the other and so finding solutions to problems.

> *A social worker was not getting all the information down accurately on forms when dealing with emergencies; her supervisor saw this as incompetence. Once the supervisor understood that she was losing her place when trying to fill out these forms quickly, the problem was solved by devising a checklist for ticking off all the items of information as she went along. More importantly, she was no longer viewed as incompetent which improved her confidence. She then related better to her supervisor and felt able to ask for help in finding solutions to new difficulties as they arose.*

The dyslexic person's strengths should also be valued and utilised.

> *One dyslexic teacher was very anxious about her own spelling. However, she taught her class her own spelling strategies - so her children were better spellers than many other children in the school. They were also more confident and independent learners because they had learned to use other resources than the teacher!*

Steps to success

Gerber, Ginsburg and Reiff (1992) identified characteristics of dyslexic adults who were highly successful in employment. They established both external and internal factors.

They identified **gaining control** as the key factor in achieving success. This means consciously deciding to "take charge of one's life" and learning how to do that. Taking control is especially necessary because of the many obstacles dyslexic people face.

Gaining control relies on three main internal characteristics:

- the **desire** to achieve and to excel

- **conscious goal setting** of both long and short-term goals

- going through a process of **reframing** or reinterpreting the experience of being dyslexic in a more positive way.

"I took O levels 14 times but I was determined to pass"

"I wanted to prove I was as good as anybody else"

"I knew I would get there even if it took me ten years"

"Dyslexia? It's part of me - I wouldn't be me without it"

Reframing involves four stages which often interact:

1) **recognition** of their difference from others and of their difficulties

"I always knew there was something wrong - why couldn't I learn like my brother?"

How Can I Help?

> "Once I understood my problems I knew what sort of help I needed"

2) **acceptance** of these differences, both the positive and negative aspects

> "I finally realised my problems weren't going to magically 'go away' - at that point I finally decided to tell my boss"

3) **understanding** of their strengths as well as their weaknesses

> "I learned to 'unpack' the disability - to see how it operated independently of me - and that gave me a lot of confidence"

> "I was going to audition for the part even if I made a fool of myself"

4) **action** taken towards their goals on the basis of understanding and in spite of fear or obstacles.

> "I knew I would have to give up my social life for three years but I was determined to get my degree"

This reframing process is apparent in every highly successful dyslexic adult; those who were moderately successful reframed as well but did not usually go through all the stages. They often had problems accepting the disability and their understanding was less complete.

> "When I took my conversion course in nursing I had to work four times harder than my colleagues - they tried to stop me because they thought I was trying to go higher than them"

The external factors in success are those activities which help in gaining control:

> "The job was great because I could dictate my reports on tape and they were relaxed about time as long as I got the work done"

- **persistence** or being prepared to work harder than anyone else

> "I had to learn anatomy by relating it to my own self-image - it was the only way I could remember where the bones and organs were"

- a **"goodness of fit"** with the environment, where they could capitalise on their strengths and have some control

> "It was finding a tutor that understood my difficulties and believed in me that kept me going"

- **"learned creativity"** or devising strategies to compensate for weaknesses and use strengths to solve problems

> "Just talking to other dyslexic people is a great help"

- the seeking and use of **support systems,** including both supportive people and opportunities to improve and develop their skills.

The authors suggest that all these factors are alterable, that it is possible to develop these characteristics which increase chances of success. Reframing particularly "seems to be a trigger mechanism" for success and for fostering the ability to find creative responses and solutions to obstacles.

However, the importance of helpful people and supportive environments should remind everyone involved in working with dyslexic young people and adults that they, too, hold one of the keys to unlocking the dyslexic individual's potential for success.

A London Language & Literacy Unit *Master*

Dyslexia: a pattern of difficulties

How can you tell if a person is dyslexic? This checklist is a quick reference, to identify indicators for further in-depth assessment. Although not exclusive, the list seeks to set out common difficulties dyslexic people may have. Individuals who are dyslexic will usually show a pattern which includes a significant number of these difficulties.

A person may be dyslexic if he/she:

- shows significant discrepancy between oral and written performance
- experiences persistent or severe problems with spelling, even with 'easy' or common words
- spells erratically - has 'good days' and 'bad days'
- has difficulty getting ideas onto paper
- has persistent problems with sentence structure, punctuation and/or organisation of written work, not due to a lack of experience
- has problems ordering things sequentially
- consistently fails to express real understanding, ideas or vocabulary in written work
- frequently misreads or miscopies
- loses place often when reading, or in a series (eg instructions)
- has difficulty in 'seeing' errors (eg proof-reading)
- finds reading new words difficult or fails to recognise familiar ones
- has handwriting which is 'messy', poorly constructed or immature
- experiences left/right confusions
- has trouble generalising, or acquiring and applying rules
- does not seem to learn by 'ordinary' teaching methods
- has a poor concept of time
- has a poor short-term memory
- mispronounces multisyllabic words
- finds it difficult to organise him/her self, work or time
- may be described as a 'quick forgetter' rather than a 'slow learner'
- has difficulty paying attention, is easily distracted visually or auditorially

demystifying DYSLEXIA

A London Language & Literacy Unit *Master*

Common features of dyslexia

Identifying problems -
how would you recognise them?

PROBLEM	INDICATOR
eg poor short term memory	**Example:** - student may forget instructions - may have difficulties with concentration - muddles up names, dates, facts
spelling	
difficulty getting ideas onto paper	
problems with sequence and order	
frequently misreading or miscopying	
losing place easily when reading	
difficulty reading new words	
failing to recognise familiar words	
left/right confusions	

demystifying DYSLEXIA

A London Language & Literacy Unit *Master*

resource sheet 2

PROBLEM	INDICATOR
trouble generalising, or acquiring and applying rules	
poor concept of time	
difficulty organising him/her self	
difficulty getting ideas onto paper	
problems finding the 'right words' when speaking	
problems finding the 'right word' when writing	

demystifying DYSLEXIA

A London Language & Literacy Unit *Master*

Am I dyslexic?

Self-check

	Yes	No
1. Do you often dial the wrong telephone number?		
2. Do you make lots of spelling mistakes?		
3. Do you have 'good days' and 'bad days' for spelling?		
4. Do you often write the date wrong?		
5. Do you get tired quickly when you read?		
6. Are you a slow reader?		
7. Do you often lose your place when you are reading?		
8. Do you often read the wrong words or find it hard to make sense of what you have read?		
9. Do you find filling out forms difficult or confusing?		
10. Do you mix up right and left?		
11. Do you mix up bus numbers?		
12. Do you have slow or messy handwriting?		
13. Do you get dates and times mixed up and miss appointments?		
14. Do you get confused with the time?		
15. Do you have difficulties taking messages on the phone?		
16. Do you forget or mix up instructions?		
17. Do you find it difficult to say the months of the year, or the alphabet, in the right order?		
18. Did you find it hard to learn your tables?		
19. Do you make mistakes when you copy from a board?		
20. Do you find it hard to organise your work, folders, time etc?		

Most dyslexic people find they have many of the above problems.

If you feel you recognise these problems in yourself, **you may be dyslexic and you might want to talk to someone about it.**

demystifying DYSLEXIA

resource sheet 3

A London Language & Literacy Unit *Master*

Identifying difficulties

Example of student's difficulties	What could be the reason?
Allegra has, since the age of 5, been educated in special schools. She is, however, well able to grasp complex issues and able to deal with abstract concepts. Her spellings are bizarre and so she has always lacked confidence with writing. Her writing is poorly formed and childish. Her reading is slow, and she relies on a sight vocabulary. Her comprehension is excellent.	
Jon is very intelligent and motivated. He has the clearest grasp of academic concepts in the group. However, his work is very messy and difficult to read. His spellings are good phonic approximations and he gets confused with homonyms. He often misreads exam questions and his general comprehension is poor, even when he rereads several times.	
Anthony finds it difficult to begin to write words which he has not practised before. Even when he knows a word, he tends to miss 'bits' out or gets letters in the wrong order. His writing is very neat, although he writes very slowly and his ideas seem jumbled. He finds reading tiring as the words have a 'halo' around them and this makes the words too bright to read for any period of time. He also frequently loses his place.	

resource sheet 4 - Activity

demystifying DYSLEXIA

A London Language & Literacy Unit Master

Dyslexic learning style: implications for learning

resource sheet 5

- holistic or 'right brain' rather than sequential or 'left brain' approaches to learning

- problems with order, sequential connections and breaking down into steps but good at seeing simultaneous connections and patterns

- difficulties in linguistic coding - inhibiting automatic processing in either the visual, phonological or motor areas when dealing with the written word

This means:

- ◆ limited strategies available for storing and retrieving language based tasks (ie putting verbal information into the long-term memory or getting it out quickly)

- ◆ a reliance on **semantic coding** or **meaning**

- ◆ a need to take an indirect or more roundabout way in dealing with language based tasks

- poor short-term memory problems (holding information, chunking, memorising facts)

This means:

- ◆ an emphasis on long-term memory involving **association of ideas and understanding:**

- easily over-loaded or distracted and inefficient verbal processing

- lack of facility and flexibility in manipulating linguistic expression and acquiring the conventions of written language

- learning from lots of specific examples and practice rather than generalisation or rules

- 'concrete' rather than 'abstract' routes to understanding

- problems with structure and organisation rather than content and ideas

---

Reliance on meaning and understanding imply:

★ a highly **personalised** approach to learning

★ a need to have the learning process and conventions made **explicit**

★ a need to understand **how** and **why**

demystifying DYSLEXIA

A London Language & Literacy Unit *Master*

Dyslexic learning style: strengths and weaknesses

Give examples of specific tasks, skills and activities which people with a right hemispheric preference would probably be good at and those which they would probably find difficult.

Then do the same for those with a left hemispheric preference.

Left hemisphere dominant

has a good short term memory

thinks in words

remembers sequences

takes in information step by step in a logical sequence

looks for cause and effect

relies on induction and analysis

is time conscious

Right hemisphere dominant

relies on highly personal associations to remember

thinks in images

remembers patterns

takes in parts in terms of whole

looks for simultaneous connections

is adept at synthesis and intuitive links

is space conscious

demystifying DYSLEXIA

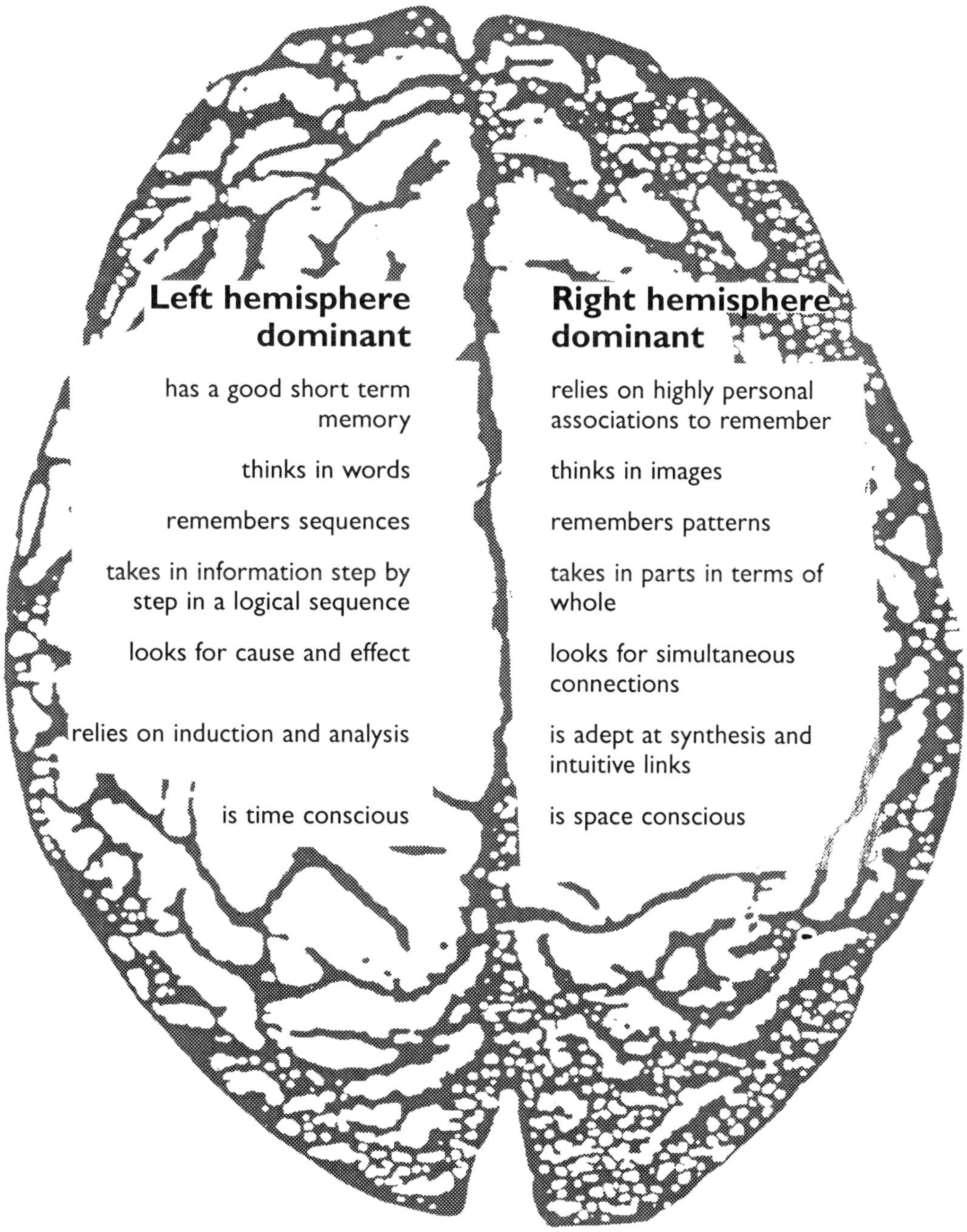

A London Language & Literacy Unit *Master*

Right hemisphere preference

good at	have problems with

Left hemisphere preference

good at	have problems with

- *Discuss what you discovered. How does it relate to your own practice?*
- *How could you help those who have a strong right hemispheric preference and are weak in left hemispheric processing?*
- *What strategies could you employ to improve learning and achievement for all learners?*

demystifying DYSLEXIA

A London Language & Literacy Unit Master

Areas of difficulty for dyslexic students

READING:
- sorting, selecting materials, reading overload
- understanding and retaining what was read
- lack of speed, extracting main points, summarising
- misreading (assignment or exam questions)
- visual stress
- understanding inferences
- reading words that are new/unfamiliar in print

SPELLING:
- interfering with written expression and vocabulary
- impeding note taking
- affecting tutor/examiner's understanding and assessment of student's work
- sometimes inhibiting writing entirely

NOTE-TAKING:
- sorting out main points
- writing and listening simultaneously
- getting enough down and reading it back
- copying quickly and correctly

WRITING:
- handwriting - poor construction /lack of speed/ interfering with getting ideas down
- written expression, sentence structure, punctuation
- planning and structuring written work
- conventions of writing, transitions between ideas, sequence
- relating abstract to particular, theory to practice
- editing and proof-reading

ORAL LANGUAGE:
- taking in information or lectures quickly enough
- misunderstanding instructions or information
- sorting what is said in a group discussion
- word-finding problems
- pronunciation of polysyllabic words

EXAMINATIONS:
- timed conditions exacerbating reading, writing and spelling problems
- memory problems affecting revision and performance
- discrepancy with coursework often resulting in considerably lower marks overall

demystifying DYSLEXIA

A London Language & Literacy Unit Master

Help in the classroom

Classroom teaching involves taking the needs of the whole group into consideration. The basic principle to remember is that students (dyslexic and non-dyslexic) will have differing learning styles, learning needs, learning difficulties and level of skills. The aim is to adopt teaching methods which meet the various needs of all the individuals in the group.

1. Present your material in a variety of ways:

★ visually:

   pictures, diagrams, use of colour coding and highlighting, good quality, well laid out handouts, practical demonstrations

★ auditorially:

   explanations, repetition, discussions, tapes, poems, stories, dialogue, drama

★ kinaesthetically:

   practical activities, three-dimensional models, excursions, making things, tactile experience and exploration

★ offer 'right brain' learning strategies:

   use of *imagery, music, drawing, visual-spatial patterns, humour, empathy* and *intuition*

   ◆ **encourage** sensory exploration and 'hands on' activities
   ◆ **develop** visualisation skills
   ◆ **encourage** imagination

2. Introduce 'holistic' ways of presenting subject matter:

★ introduce the 'whole picture' and **then** the parts within it

★ make explicit links from particular examples to the general overall idea

★ give **concrete** examples (using audio-visual aids or demonstrations where possible) to build up a 'picture' of abstract ideas

demystifying DYSLEXIA

3. Discuss the learning process with your students:

explain why you are doing a particular activity

- which skills are you hoping to develop?
- what information or skill is the student expected to learn?
- what is the relationship to other learning experiences?

discuss with students how they intend to go about learning something

- explore which strategies have worked for them
- encourage students to share strategies which have been successful
- develop students' analytic skills to decide why certain strategies work and others are less successful

help them realise the necessity and value of practice in acquiring a new skill

- discuss how memory works and the importance of the motor memory
- relate new learning to successful learning in the past

encourage them to make their own meaningful connections to what they are learning

- 'study tapes' - information recorded over music which is meaningful to the student
- mnemonics which are personally meaningful
- 'picture stories' either in imagination or on paper in order to remember facts or events
- 'mind maps', 'spidergrams' or drawings to plan essays

4. Encourage students to take charge of their own learning:

offer a **variety** of methods and approaches for them to select or discover which works best for them

set up **active learning** situations where they can explain or demonstrate things to each other, work in pairs or groups, select activities or projects, set goals

stress **self-checking** and give plenty of opportunity for self-assessment

A London Language & Literacy Unit Master

5. Introduce learning skills through *content*:

discuss, define, explain and demonstrate language particular to your subject: common vocabulary, new terminology, expressions, jargon or idioms

break down processes into steps with **opportunity for feedback** to check understanding and develop language skills

encourage students to **ask questions**: questions are a way of checking our hypothesis about what's being presented

give students opportunities to **observe models**: give them examples of what they should be aiming for

demonstrate and **explain** how to do assignments

6. Offer specific help with:

Note taking:

- make your own notes available
- write main points and terminology on board
- when using OHPs - type information, summarise main points; don't put too much information onto sheet
- make handouts clear and easily accessible
- use mind maps and simplified diagrams

Reading:

- give guidance on selected key works (especially articles which are clearly structured and well presented) to minimise reading load
- identify new subject vocabulary in texts
- offer audio-visual sources on subject matter, eg OU programmes, TV documentaries or discussions, videos - these can help with structure as well as content

Writing:

- offer models of written work; essays; reports; projects
- give help with planning, structure, organisation

Be specific and practical

Write everything down clearly

Don't expect student to remember without extra reinforcement or secure framework

demystifying DYSLEXIA

A London Language & Literacy Unit Master

focus on

- ◆ conventions: introduction, sub-headings, conclusion
- ◆ identifying main points
- ◆ identifying relevant data and what is irrelevant
- ◆ selection and inclusion of quotations/references
- ◆ ordering points and making transitions between points
- ◆ presentation (encouraging the use of computer when presenting assignments or essays)

7. Generally:

- ★ Make sure instructions are clear and written down for student to check
- ★ Be *explicit* in expectations
- ★ Help students to formulate questions
- ★ Be clear in your own communications and check understanding
- ★ Be aware of the extra time, effort and concentration the dyslexic student needs to bring to tasks involving language

8. Finally, remember:

- ★ Some students can only generalise from lots of specific concrete examples and practice
- ★ When a student makes an error in a sequence you may need to retrace *all* the steps with them rather than just point out where they went wrong
- ★ Some students may be easily distracted by noise, activity or visual 'clutter'
- ★ Dyslexic students may need more time to absorb information - try to break up learning sessions, discussions and activities to allow this processing to happen
- ★ The final stage of learning is being able to 'teach' someone else - make opportunities for students to do this (through talking, writing, demonstrations, presentations)

A London Language & Literacy Unit *Master*

How can I help?

Case studies

Case Study 1 -

Sharon has no difficulties with the content of her course, showing a lively and intelligent interest in all aspects of it and enjoying discussions. However, she finds reading difficult as she quickly gets very tired, her eyes water and burn and she has trouble remembering what she has read. She has some difficulty with planning and organising her assignments, but her main problem with written work is that her spelling is poor (she tends to spell the way she thinks the word sounds) and she frequently rubs out words which she thinks she has misspelled. This makes the writing of assignments very slow. She enjoys most of her lectures, except for maths, which she loathes. Not only can she not follow what is said, she cannot read information from the board quickly enough and gets headaches from being in the lesson.

1. *What do you think is the nature of Sharon's difficulties?*
2. *What seems to be Sharon's preferred learning mode?*
3. *What strategies can you adopt within the classroom to make the reading process easier for Sharon?*
4. *Is there any equipment you could order to help Sharon with getting information from texts?*
5. *How could she be helped in the maths lesson?*
6. *How could you help Sharon improve her assignment writing?*

Case Study 2 -

Jenny frequently 'muddles up' spoken or written instructions and gets the 'wrong end of the stick'. Her written work is poor, as her spellings are often bizarre and it is difficult to understand what she is saying. She finds it extremely difficult to express her ideas on paper, especially when needing to write factual explanations or reports, although she is able to write vivid and imaginative fiction. She has difficulties expressing herself as she frequently cannot retrieve the correct word she wants to use, or mispronounces words when she is speaking. As a result she is very withdrawn and hates to participate in class room discussions.

1. *What do you thin is the nature of Jenny's language processing difficulties?*
2. *What do you think might be Jenny's preferred mode of learning?*

demystifying DYSLEXIA

3. What methods/strategies could be used within the classroom to help Jenny understand and remember assignments?

4. How could Jenny be helped to improve her spelling?

5. How could you enable Jenny to be more confident in class discussions?

6. What strategies could be used to develop Jenny's written language skills?

Case Study 3 -

Mark is extremely articulate in class discussion and very quick to grasp concepts. Although Mark's assignment work generally conforms to the standards of the course, his difficulties become very marked under examination conditions. In these cases, his handwriting deteriorates to such an extent, that it becomes illegible and his spelling is also affected to a far greater degree than normal. He finds it difficult to organise himself and his work, his assignments are often full of ideas but "all tangled up" and disjointed and these difficulties are exacerbated during exams. He appears to be a confident and fluent reader but complains that he often cannot understand what he has read and frequently loses his place.

1. What do you think is the nature of Mark's language processing difficulties?

2. What do you think is Mark's preferred learning mode?

3. How can tutors help Mark to realise his potential in examinations?

4. What strategies could be used to help Mark improve his writing skills?

5. What strategies might help Mark improve his reading comprehension?

A London Language & Literacy Unit Master

How can I help?

Supporting students

Student Problems	Possible Reason	Strategies for Helping: Classroom or Learning Support
1. The student cannot take notes from lectures or copy quickly or accurately from the board so isn't getting the information down. He can't read back the notes he does take.		
2. The student's work is messy, his handwriting is difficult to read with lots of crossing out and misspellings. His work is poorly organised and he is often late, forgets the piece of work he is meant to bring or brings the wrong piece and loses his papers. It looks as if he doesn't bother.		

demystifying DYSLEXIA

A London Language & Literacy Unit *Master*

Student Problems	Possible Reason	Strategies for Helping: Classroom or Learning Support
3. The student has difficulties getting information from texts for assignments and often misunderstands written instructions. When given reading to do she takes much longer than the other students.		
4. The student is very articulate in class and seems to heve a good grasp of the subject but avoids written work and what she does hand in is late and of very poor standard.		
5. The student doesn't seem to pay attention in lectures and forgets instructions or gets them wrong. He also seems to have difficulty participating in group discussions even though in individual tutorials he seems to understand the subject.		

demystifying DYSLEXIA

A London Language & Literacy Unit Master

How can I help:

Student Writing

Use the selections of student writing below as a basis for discussion.

- *What problems do you observe? What strengths?*
- *What sort of support do you think each student needs?*
- *What aspects or difficulties would you prioritise to work on?*
- *Can you suggest approaches or strategies for classroom and/or learning support for each student?*

Student A (first draft of an essay)

> the value of Exercise
> Exercise increase circlation and increase Oxegen intake
> It allsow ferms the mucale's and makes you sopple.
> it can help delay some ageing simtom's.
> It is difficult to find the right exercise. Thair is so many. You must find one that sout you
> it dusn'te have to be strenuse. slowly is the way.
> Exercise must be part of your daily rutine.
> ~~■ ■ ■ ■ ■~~
> Slowly your dBody will become able to do evey movement early.
> Exercise don't alter your wieght it helps to toning and tightining the body's outer layers of mucale's.
> ~~■ ■ ■ ■~~
> the more exercise you do the better your heath and energe and vitalte.

demystifying DYSLEXIA

A London Language & Literacy Unit Master

Student B (written under timed conditions)

> When a farmer decides on what grasses to use clover and seed mixture it depend because the farmer has the idea of the land which he perhaps covered last year and he is trying to put a good example about seed mixture he's going to rake over the field perhaps has done poor over last new years, cattle grazing want think about them and there ability where they would likely to graze

When a farmer decides on what grasses like clover and seed mixture it depend because the farmer has the idea of the land which he perhaps covered last year and he is trying to put a good example about seed mixture he's going to rake over the field perhaps has done poor over the last few years, cattle grazing wasn't think about them and their ability where they would likely to graze.

demystifying DYSLEXIA

A London Language & Literacy Unit *Master*

Routes to training & education

Things to consider

How is the course delivered?

- lectures?
- practical work?
- a range of activities?

What will assignments require?

- how much reading? at what level?
- what kind of writing is required? how much?
- can a word processor be used?

What are the methods of assessment?

- course work based?
- exam based?
- practical skills based?
- are alternatives methods of assessment acceptable?

What support is available?

- extra tutorial help?
- specialist dyslexia support?
- access to or personal use of equipment?
- special examination provision?

demystifying DYSLEXIA

A London Language & Literacy Unit *Master*

How can I help?

Employment, training and careers: case studies

a) Dawn is 21 years old and has been working as a helper in a local playgroup. She loves working with children and the playgroup leader thinks very highly of the way she relates to the children. She seems very bright and eager to learn. Dawn would like to become a nursery nurse and has decided to apply to do an NNEB Course. However, her writing skills are very limited and her spelling is extremely poor. She has just been diagnosed as dyslexic, with moderately severe auditory processing difficulties.

b) Richard is a 17 year old who likes messing around with machines and building things. He is able to fix almost anything that is broken and is also good at computer games. He played truant a lot at school and was very skilled at avoiding any writing although he liked drawing. He also avoided taking any exams by not going back to school after the Easter holidays. Now Richard has turned up at his local FE college with a friend to "check out what they have to offer". You suspect he might be dyslexic.

c) Mary is a mature woman who has been doing a fairly routine office job successfully for several years. Since being diagnosed dyslexic two years ago, she has gained the confidence to get a GCSE in geography at grade B. Now part of the work she did is no longer needed so she is having to take on new work of a secretarial nature. This means she not only has to use a keyboard but also has to organise and prioritise her workload. Her new superviser claims that Mary makes too many silly mistakes, refuses to prioritise work and her desk is chaotic. Mary needs her job but is beginning to find it intolerable.

- *How would you advise*
  a) Dawn,
  b) Richard
  c) Mary?

- *What questions would you ask?*

- *What information would you give?*

- *What issues would you need to address?*

- *What advice would you offer?*

- *What further action would you take?*

demystifying DYSLEXIA

A London Language & Literacy Unit *Master*

Twenty questions

Q: Why is diagnosis necessary?

To diagnose a person as dyslexic indicates a positive way of understanding the individual's problem and potential. Without being aware of the nature of language processing difficulties, students' errors and behaviour are likely to be misunderstood and mislabelled and teaching is unlikely to be geared appropriately to the dyslexic learning style. For most dyslexic individuals, a diagnosis is a liberating experience, enabling them to get appropriate support, make constructive life plans and positive decisions about their future lives.

Q: Should people be 'labelled' dyslexic?

Dyslexia has begun to have a positive image, with dyslexic people being able to identify with famous men and women who became successful in the fields of politics, art, acting. literature, science and sport.

Most dyslexic people have already been labelled as "stupid"; "thick" or "lazy". Some were 'diagnosed' as being "educationally sub-normal" and now hold good honours degrees. Most people who have persistent difficulties with written language are relieved to know that there is a name for the condition which has adversely affected their lives and to know they are not alone.

Q: Are there degrees of dyslexia?

Yes. Some dyslexic people continue to find it difficult to read and write. Others learn to read but find spelling and writing problems limit their achievement. Students in higher education who have battled their way through the language requirements of an A' Level examination may still have difficulty in telling the time, copying accurately, organising their essays or taking lecture notes.

Q. Are there types of dyslexia?

Yes. Dyslexia is a "veritable syndrome" of difficulties and the continuum of indicators makes definition of the condition difficult. However, specific areas of processing difficulties can be identified: visual processing difficulties, auditory processing difficulties, difficulties with motor co-ordination and integration.

Q: What makes dyslexic learners different from slow learners?

Slow learners do not exhibit the same discrepancy between their intelligence and their written expression or between verbal and non-verbal abilities. Many slow learners can spell and write adequately, but have difficulties with concepts. The dyslexic student often understands a lot and usually has many ideas, but finds it difficult to "get them out", especially on paper.

Dyslexic students usually make good progress after having followed a structured programme of work based on their specific needs and learning style, whereas slow learners make slow progress. The dyslexic learner might be described as a 'quick forgetter' rather than a slow learner.

demystifying DYSLEXIA

A London Language & Literacy Unit *Master*

Q: Are we giving people diagnosed as dyslexic an unfair advantage in education and work?

No. The term 'Equal Opportunities' means that each individual has the opportunity to maximise their potential in life. Dyslexic young people and adults often missed out on educational opportunities while at school precisely because they were not diagnosed or given specific teaching appropriate to their needs. If these needs continue to be ignored, then once again they are at a disadvantage. Dyslexic people have proved that they are well able to succeed in occupations where their talents and abilities and personal compensating strategies may be used.

Q: Surely there must be some emotional problems?

Yes. Literacy is a high status skill in our society and one which all members are expected to acquire. Dyslexic people usually have a history of failure and mis-labelling so they often suffer from a lack of self-confidence, low self-image and esteem. Problems with literacy at work or college may cause depression, anger and frustration, especially if they know they are intellectually capable of doing the job or course. However, emotional problems are the result of being dyslexic, not the cause.

Q: Is it hereditary?

Studies have shown there is almost definitely a hereditary factor. However, this does not mean that reading problems are fixed and there is nothing to be done about them - reading and writing can be taught and improved!

Q: I thought dyslexia was "word blindness"?

This term was coined by James Hinshelwood who in 1917 published a book *Congenital Word Blindness*. Although his research has proved very valuable in the study of dyslexia, this term is no longer acceptable because it is too limited in its description. Dyslexia is not primarily a visual problem even if there are visual processing difficulties. Also, many dyslexic people can read.

Q: Is it to do with left handedness?

There may be a small correlation. It is generally true that a right handed person usually has a left-hemisphere control of language, but so do the majority of left handed people. However, sensory and motor mechanisms on one side of the body tend to be controlled by the opposite side of the brain; therefore control of functions such as writing by left-handed people may be slowed down by messages having to refer to both hemispheres or cross from one hemisphere to another and back again, increasing processing time. There is some suggestion that dyslexia has to do with mixed laterality, eg being right eyed, left handed and right footed.

demystifying DYSLEXIA

A London Language & Literacy Unit *Master*

Q: Does it affect men more than women?

Dyslexia has always been regarded as afflicting males four times more than females. However, recent research both in America and Britain has suggested that dyslexia may affect both sexes more equally. The reasons for this discrepancy is thought to be that boys are more likely to display secondary behavioural problems which result in referral to educational psychologists and that parents and teachers are more concerned with the scholastic progress of boys than girls. Also, boys generally develop language skills later than girls, so problems in boys may be more apparent at an early stage.

Q. Is it a disability?

Yes. According to the 1981 Education Act, "a child has special educational needs if he has a learning difficulty which calls for special educational provision to be made for him. A child has a 'learning difficulty' if he has a significantly greater difficulty in learning than the majority of children....". It is also recognised as a disability for the purposes of employment and by the Further and Higher Education Councils for the purposes of disability grants and additional support.

Q. Can it be cured?

No, it is not a disease; but it can be minimised through early intervention and by developing strategies for dealing with weaknesses. It is an ongoing difficulty which will continue to affect certain aspects of the person's life. This is why counselling and the adoption of compensating strategies is so important.

Q. Are people who claim they are dyslexic merely attention seekers?

People with dyslexic difficulties are often very frustrated and confused about their abilities. They know something is wrong but not what and they have usually suffered greatly from misunderstanding and negative labelling. They are not so much seeking attention as understanding. In fact, they are often very diffident. If they have not received appropriate teaching, then they are entitled to demand the type of education which they have been denied in the past.

Q: Is it a middle-class excuse?

Dyslexia affects people irrespective of race, gender or class. It has been perceived as a middle-class condition because much of the specialist educational provision for dyslexic children is available in the private education sector. Many children in the state sector are denied appropriate help with their written language difficulties because of inadequate specialist provision available due to budgetary considerations, lack of knowledge about the condition, low expectations or teachers refusing to recognise that such a condition exists.

Q: Does it affect one ethnic group more than another?

If dyslexia is a syndrome which affects the processing of language, then persons within all ethnic groups may be affected. The difficulties manifest themselves more noticeably in written languages which are not alphabetically consistent. English is a prime example of one such language and problems of dyslexia are more obvious in countries where these languages are used. However, it will show up in all languages and in all cultures.

demystifying DYSLEXIA

A London Language & Literacy Unit *Master*

Q: Do dyslexic people have difficulties with maths?

There is often a correlation between difficulties with written language and difficulties with maths where sequencing, directional and memorisation problems are evident. These often reveal themselves particularly in long division and algebra. Some dyslexic people may be very good at maths, using skills for seeing patterns and visualising, rather than calculation. Sometimes the difficulties are really with the language of maths rather than the essential concepts.

Q. Can word processors help dyslexic people?

Some dyslexic individuals, particularly those with motor integration problems, certainly benefit from using a word processor as it by-passes the interference which poor motor co-ordination puts in the way of their spelling and writing. Spell checks maybe useful to enable the presentation of work which reflects abilities and not spelling difficulties. Organisational difficulties are greatly helped by being able to move text around the screen. However, although significant improvements in writing are often made, word processors do not automatically correct errors between homonyms, punctuation or expression. also, effective use of word processors depends on the acquisition of good keyboard skills.

Q Are dyslexic people often artistic?

Yes, as many dyslexic people have a cognitive style which relies on a preference for right brain functioning. The right hemisphere of the brain is the side which processes spatially rather then temporally. Using the right hemisphere we understand images, have leaps of insight, are spontaneous without necessarily being logical or sequential and see patterns and simultaneous interconnections. Many people in the creative or artistic professions have such a cognitive style; they perceive the world and express themselves most easily in pictures and images rather than using language to express their ideas.

Q How can someone with visual processing problems be good at drawing?

Spelling and drawing are two different activities which utilise different parts of the brain. Language based tasks are primarily processed in the left hemisphere, whereas drawing requires more activity in the right hemisphere. The memory of spellings relies on remembering sequences of abstract symbols representing speech sounds; drawing relies on remembering interconnected visual-spatial patterns.

demystifying DYSLEXIA

Glossary

ACUITY - the sharpness or acuteness of an image or sound.

ACQUIRED DYSLEXIA - loss of ability to read (and spell) through brain damage as distinguished from developmental dyslexia, which is a failure to learn to read or spell.

AGRAPHIA - decline or loss of the ability to write.

ALEXIA - loss of ability to read because of some brain damage, such as a cerebral stroke. The term also refers to the complete failure to acquire reading skills as well as to a partial or complete loss of these skills through damage.

ANGULAR GYRUS - part of the brain which associates the visual form of word with the corresponding auditory pattern from Wernicke's area. Important in written language functions.

ANOMIA - difficulty in recalling or remembering words or the names of objects.

APHASIA - defect or loss of power of expression by speech, writing or signs, or of comprehending spoken or written language due to injury or disease of the brain.

APRAXIA - inability to carry out purposeful movements in the absence of paralysis.

ARCUATE FASCICULUS - a long bundle of nerve fibres which links the receptive and expressive language areas.

BROCA'S APHASIA - an expressive or non-fluent aphasia, which is often characterised by 'telegraphic' speech; results from a lesion to Broca's area.

BROCA'S AREA - (situated in frontal lobe) area of brain used for expressive language - evokes programme for articulation.

CAT SCANS (Computerised tomography) - an x-ray procedure in which a computer draws a map from the measured densities of the brain and provides a three dimensional representation of the brain.

CEREBRAL DOMINANCE - the control of activities by the brain, for certain functions. In most individuals, the left side of the brain controls language function, and the left is considered the dominant hemisphere for this activity.

COGNITION - a general term used to refer to the processes involved in thinking and knowing.

CORPUS COLLOSUM - a system of nerve fiber systems which connects the areas of the two hemispheres. Split brain patients are those whose corpus collosum has been severed.

DEVELOPMENTAL DYSLEXIA - a severe difficulty with the written form of laguage independent of intellectual, cultural and emotional causation. It is characterised by a discrepancy between an individual's written language skills and their intelligence and chronological age.

DIRECTIONALITY - an awareness of the relative position of one side of the body versus the other.

DYSCALCULIA - difficulty in performing arithmetical operations.

Glossary

DYSGRAPHIA - a difficulty in performing the motor-movement required for handwriting or in integrating the motor-function with writing and spelling. The condition is often associated with neurological dysfunction.

FRONTAL LOBE - an area of the brain where higher thinking processes, intellectual activity and conscious intention occur.

GRAPHEME - refers to a pictorial or graphic unit of a written word, eg letters or written symbols.

GRAPHEMIC READING - when the meaning of a word is derived from the picture that it makes as a whole rather than by sounding out the syllables.

KINAESTHETIC - relating to the perception of movement or of the position of the limbs and the body.

LATERALITY - the side of the brain that controls a given function; hence studies of laterality are devoted to determining which side of the brain controls various functions, eg handedness.

LATERALISATION - the process whereby functions come to be located primarily on one side of the brain.

LESION - any damage to the nervous system.

LEXICON - a dictionary, or memory store in the brain that contains words and their meanings.

LOGOGRAPHIC - a symbolic representation of a meaning, part of a word or a whole word, eg %, £, $. Used to refer to the first stage of reading whereby words are identified by pictorial features.

MAGNETIC RESONANCE IMAGING (MRI) - an imaging procedure in which a computer draws a map from the measured changes in the magnetic resonance of atoms in the brain.

MATURATIONAL-LAG HYPOTHESIS - explanation of a disability that suggests that a system is not yet mature or is maturing slowly.

MOTOR INTEGRATION - written language skills require automatic integration between the auditory areas of the brain, the visual-spatial areas of the brain and rapid signals arriving to the brain from the muscles and joints in the body. Dysfunction in any part of these complex signals will prevent smooth functioning of expressive language.

MORPHEME - a language element which has a meaning or grammatical function which cannot be sub-divided, eg trust is a one-morpheme word: trustful, a two morpheme word.

MYELINATION - the formation of myelin (a substance which forms an insulating sheath around certain nerve fibers). Myelination in the corpus collosum is the last to occur.

OCCIPITAL LOBES - a general area of the cortex lying in the back part of the head.

ORTHOGRAPHIC - relating to the writing system. Used by Uta Frith to describe the third stage of reading based on visual and lexical word recognition, independent of sound.

PARIETAL LOBE - an area of the brain which constitutes the primary body sense area, and where logical grammatical relationships are processed and simultaneous complex spatial syntheses formed.

Glossary

PERCEPTION - the process by which an organism interprets information from the external world resulting from activity in the various sensory regions of the neo-cortex which have begun in primary sensory receptors.

PERSEVERATION - tendency to repeatedly emit the same verbal or motor response to a stimuli, eg in handwriting to repeat letters or letter patterns.

PHONEME - a sound element or unit of a word which cannot be broken down further. As words can be analysed into graphemes or morphemes, they can also be analysed into phonemes.

PHONICS - a method of teaching people to read through the emphasis of teaching letter-sound relationships and emphasising the role of sound in decoding the written word.

PHONOLOGICAL - refers to the sound system of a language. Phonological processes refer to analysing and synthesising speech sounds in spoken or written language.

PLANUM TEMPORALE - the cortical area behind the auditory cortex.

PREFERRED COGNITIVE MODE - the preferred use of one type of thought process in preference to another, for example, using the visuospatial instead of verbal. Sometimes attributed to the assumed superior functioning of one hemisphere over the other.

PRIMARY AUDITORY AREA - receives words as sensation from the ears.

SACCADE - is a 'reading launch' during which the eyes make rapid jerks to move along a line of text.

SCOTOPIC SENSITIVITY SYNDROME - a difficulty in reading texts caused by a dysfunction of the visual system characterised by a sensitivity to certain light sources, luminance and colour contrasts.

SEMANTIC - relates to the meanings of words and symbols.

SENSORIMOTOR - a term applied to the combination of the input of sensations and the output of motor activity.

SYNTACTIC - relating to the grammar system of a language and the linguistic rules of word order including the function of words in a sentence.

TELESCOPING - a tendency to make words shorter when spelling due to the omission of syllables.

TEMPORAL LOBE - area of the brain where analysis and synthesis of sound occur, and where time or temporal sense is processed.

VISUAL CORTEX - situated in the occipital lobe and the primary visual area for receptive symbolic language and visual information.

WERNICKE'S APHASIA - a speech disorder in which a person articulates words in a language-like fashion, but what is said actually makes little sense.

WERNICKE'S AREA - area of brain which controls receptive language. Processes words: is used for understanding speech, phonemic discrimination and organisation of grammatical structures for sentences.

References:

Adams, Marilyn Jager (1990) *Beginning to Read: Thinking and Learning about Print* Massachusetts Institute of Technology

Armstrong, Thomas (1994) *Multiple Intelligences in the Classroom* Alexandria, Virginia, Association for Supervision and Curriculum Development

Baddeley, Alan (1986) *Working Memory* Oxford, Clarendon

Bakker, D ((1976) *Perceptual Asymmetries and Reading Proficiency* Amsterdam: Paedologisch Instituut Research Report No 2

Beard, Roger (1993) *Teaching Literacy, Balancing Perspectives* London, Hodder & Stoughton

Benton, A and Pearl, D (1979). *Dyslexia: An Appraisal of Current Knowledge* Oxford University Press

Bradley, Lynette (1990) "Rhyming Connections in Learning to Read and Spell" in *Children's Difficulties in Reading, Spelling and Writing* **Pumfrey, P and Elliott, C** Basingstoke, The Falmer Press

Bryant, P & Bradley, L (1985): *Children's reading problems: psychology and education* Oxford, Blackwell

Bryant, P E., and Bradley, L. (1980) "Why children sometimes write words which they cannot read" in *Cognitive Processes in Spelling:* **U Frith** (ed) London: Academic Press

Bertelson, Paul ed.(1987) *The Onset of Literacy* The MIT Press

Caine, Renate and Caine, Geoffrey (1991) *Making Connections: Teaching and the Human Brain* Alexandria, Virginia; Association for Supervision and Curriculum Development

Chasty, H (1981) "What is Dyslexia? A Developmental Language Perspective" in *Children's Written Language Difficulties* **Snowling M J** (1985) ed Windsor, NFER - Nelson

Chasty, H and Friel J (1991) *Children with Special Needs: Assessment, Law and Practice. Caught in the Act* London, Jessica Kingsley Publishers

Critchley, M (1970) *The Dyslexic Child* London, Heinemann

Critchley, M and Critchley, E A (1978) *Dyslexia Defined* London, Heinemann

De Hirsch, K., Jansky, J. and Langford, W D. (1966) *Predicting Reading Failure* New York: Harper and Row

Dunn, R (1978) *Teaching Students Through Their Individual Learning Styles: A Practical Approach* Reston, Va: Reston Publishing Company

Edwards, Betty (1981) *Drawing on the Right Side of the Brain* Fontana/Collins

Ellis, Andrew W (1984) *Reading, Writing and Dyslexia: A Cognitive Analysis* Lawrence Erlbaum Associates

Frith, Uta ed.(1980) *Cognitive Processes in Spelling* London, Academic Press

Galaburda, A M (1983) "Developmental Dyslexia: Current Anatomical Research" in *Annals of Dyslexia*, vol 33 pp 41-53

Gardner, H (1987) "The Theory of Multiple Intelligences" in *Annals of Dyslexia*, vol. 37 pp 19-35

Gerber, Paul J, Ginsberg, Rick and Reiff, Henry (1992) "Identifying Alterable Patterns in Employment Success for Highly Successful Adults with Learning Disabilities" in *Journal of Learning Disabilities* Vol 25, No 8, October 1992

References

Geschwind, Norman (1982) "Why Orton was Right" in *Annals of Dyslexia*, vol 32, Orton Dyslexia Society, reprint 98

Geschwind, Norman and A M Galaburda eds (1984) *Cerebral Dominance: The Biological Foundations* Cambridge Mass, Harvard University

Glover, John A, Ronning, Royce R and Bruning, Roger H (1990) *Cognitive Psychology for Teachers* New York, Macmillan Publishing Co

Hallgren, B (1950) "Specific Dyslexia (Congenital Word Blindness): A clinical and genetic study" in *Acta Psychiatrica ex Neurologica 5* p 153 Supplement 65

Harris, M and Coltheart (1986) *Language Processing in Children and Adults* Routledge & Kegan Paul

Hinshelwood, James (1917) *Congenital Word Blindness* London: H K Lewis

Hulme, Charles (1981) *Reading Retardation and Multi-Sensory Reading* London, Routledge & Kegan Paul

Irlen, Helen (1991) *Reading by the Colors (Overcoming Dyslexia and Other Reading Disabilities through the Irlen Method)* New York, Avery Publishing Group

Jansky, J and de Hirsch, K (1972) *Preventing Reading Failure* New York, Harper and Row

Jorm, A.F. (1983) *The Psychology of Reading and Spelling* London, Reutledge & Kegan Paul

Klein, Cynthia and Millar, Robin (1990) *Unscrambling Spelling*, London, Hodder and Stoughton

Klein, Cynthia (1991) *Setting up a Learning Programme for Dyslexic Adults* Language and Literacy Unit

Klein Cynthia (1992) *Diagnosing Dyslexia* Basic Skills Agency

Kolb, Bryan and Whishaw, Ian Q (1990) *Fundamentals of Human Neuropsychology* New York, W H Freeman and Company

Kolb, David (1984) *Learning by Discovery* Englewood Cliffs, New Jersey Prentice-Hall

Leong C.K. (1981) *Children with Specific Reading Difficulty* Bv Amsterdam, Swets & Zeitlinger

Levy, J ((1982) "Children Think with their Whole Brains" in *Student Learning Styles and Brain Behaviour* National Association of Secondary School Principals

Lovegrove, W (1991) "Spatial frequency processing in normal and dyslexic readers" in *Visual Dyslexia* vol 13 **Stein J** (ed)

McLoughlin D, Fitzgibbon G, Young V (1994) *Adult Dyslexia - Assessment, Counselling and Training"* London, Whurr Publishers

Morgan, Pringle (1986) "A Case of Congenital Word Blindness" in *British Medical Journal*, No 7

Nathes, T (1974) *Understanding Dyslexia* London, Pewry Press

Orton, S T (1925) *Wordblindness in School Children* Archives of Neurology and Psychiatry 14

Paulides, George, ed (1990) *Perspectives in Dyslexia: Volume 2 Cognitive Language and Treatment* New York, John Wiley & Sons

Peer, Lindsay (June 1994) from a talk, London

Pumfrey, Peter and Elliott, Colin eds (1990) *Children's Difficulties in Reading, Spelling and Writing* Basingstoke, The Falmer Press

Pumfrey, Peter and Reason, Rea (1993) *Specific Learning Difficulties (Dyslexia): Challenges and Responses* London, Routledge

References

Reid, Gavin (1994) *Specific Learning Difficulties (Dyslexia): A Handbook for Study and Practice* Edinburgh, Moray House Institute of Education

Rutter, M (1978) "Prevalence and Types of Dyslexia" in *Dyslexia: An Appraisal of Current Knowledge* **Benton, A and Pearl, D** (eds) New York, Oxford University Press

Satz, P and Morris, R (1981) "Learning disability subtypes: A review" in *Neuropsychological and Cognitive Processes in Reading.* **Pirozzolo and C Wittrock** (eds) New York: Academic Press

Satz P, Taylor H G, Friel J and Fletcher J M (1978) "Some developmental and predictive pre-cursors of reading disabilities: a six year follow up" in *Dyslexia: An Appraisal of Current Knowledge* **Benton A L and Pearl D** (eds) New York, Oxford University Press

Snowling, M J (ed) (1985) *Children's' Written Language Difficulties* Windsor, NFER-Nelson

Snowling, M (1987) *Dyslexia: A Cognitive Developmental Perspective* Oxford, Basil Blackwell

Snowling & Thomson ed (1991) *Dyslexia: Integrating Theory and Practice* London, Whurr Publishers

Sperry, R (1973) "Lateral Specialisation of Cerebral Function in the Surgically Separated Hemispheres" in *The Psychophysiology of Thinking* **McGuigan F J and Schoonover R A** (eds) NY Academic Press

Springer & Deutsch (1989) *Left Brain: Right Brain* New York, W.H. Freeman and Company

Stein, J F (1991) "Hemispheric Specialisation and Dyslexia" in *Reading and Writing, an Interdisciplinary Journal 4: 1991*

Stein, J & Fowler (1991) "Vision and Language" in *Dyslexia - Integrating Theory and Practice* op cit

Tallal, P (1991) Quoted in the *New York Times*; September 15th 1991

Tarnopol, Lester and Tarnopol, Muriel eds (1977) *Brain Function and Reading Disabilities* Baltimore, University Park Press

Thomson, Michael E (1990) *Developmental Dyslexia* London, Whurr Publishers

Vellutino, Frank (1981) *Dyslexia: Theory and Research* Cambridge, Massachusetts Institute of Technology

Vellutino, F R and Scanlon, D M (1987) "Phonological Coding, Phonological Awareness and Reading Ability: Evidence for a longitudinal and experimental study" in *Merrill-Palmer Quarterly 33*

Vygotsky, Lev (1939) "Thought and Speech" in *Psychiatry II*

Vygotsky, Lev (1962) *Thought and Language* Cambridge, Massachusetts Institute of Technology

West, Thomas G (1991) *In the Mind's Eye - Visual Thinkers Gifted People with Learning Difficulties,. Computer Images and the Ironies of Creativity* Buffalo, New York, Prometheus Books

Recommended Reading and Resources

General Reading

Edwards, Janice (1994) *The Scars of Dyslexia*, Cassell Research (Moving studies of experiences of being dyslexic)

Gilroy, D (1993) Compiled by. *Dyslexia and Higher Education*. Bangor Dyslexia Unit (Useful for those thinking of, or entering higher education)

McLoughlin D, Fitzgibbon, G and Young, V (1994) *Adult Dyslexia - Assessment, Counselling and Training* Whurr Publishers (Useful chapters on assessment and careers guidance and counselling)

Miles, T and Miles E (1990) *Dyslexia - 100 years* OU Press (Provides a good overview and discussion of issues and debates surrounding the concept of dyslexia)

Miles, T and Miles E eds (1992) *Dyslexia and Mathematics* Routledge (A collection of writing on various aspects of maths, including assessment and strategies, primarily aimed at older children - but useful for those working with adults as well)

Miles, T and Gilroy, D (1986) *Dyslexia at College* Methuen (Focuses on university students with useful ideas and suggestions for study skills, with some interesting personal accounts)

Miles, T and Varma, V eds (1995) *Dyslexia and Stress* Whurr Publishers (A series of chapters on stress in dyslexic people of different ages and various circumstances)

Osmond, J (1993) *The Reality of Dyslexia* Cassell Educational Ltd (Very good on the experience of dyslexia and includes a chapter on adults)

Pumfrey, P and Reason, R (1992) *Specific Learning Difficulties (Dyslexia): Challenges and Responses* NFER- Nelson (Excellent for a review of the literature and research on dyslexia, along with a comprehensive review of policy and practice)

Snowling M and Thomson M eds(1991) *Dyslexia: Integrating Theory and Practice* Whurr Publishers. (Selection of papers from the Second International Conference of the British Dyslexia Association, focusing on a wide range of issues including definitions, research and teaching)

West, Thomas G (1991) *In the Mind's Eye: Visual Thinkers, Gifted People with Learning Difficulties, Computer Images and the Ironies of Creativity* Prometheus Books (Fascinating accounts of the link between creativity and dyslexia)

Theory and Research

Ellis, A (1984) *Reading, Writing and Dyslexia: A Cognitive Analysis* Laurence Erlbaum (Presents useful models of language processing which address specific aspects of reading and writing and examines acquired and developmental dyslexia)

Frith, U ed (1980) *Cognitive Processes in Spelling* Academic Press (A comprehensive exploration of research, theory and practice, including Frith's model of the stages in the acquisition of written language)

Glover, J, Ronning, R and Bruning, R (1990) *Cognitive Psychology for Teachers* MacMillan

Recommended reading and resources

Publishing Company (Though not specifically about dyslexia, extremely useful research into writing and reading difficulties and practical strategies)

Harris, M and Coltheart, Max (1986) *Language Processing in Children and Adults* Routledge (Research in cognitive psychology including acquired dyslexia)

Irlen, H (1991) *Reading by the Colours: Overcoming Dyslexia and Other Reading Disabilities Through the Irlen Method* Avery Publishing Group (Explains scotopic sensitivity syndrome, its relation to dyslexia and the use of coloured filters to help with reading difficulties)

Jorm, A F (1983) *The Psychology of Spelling and Reading Difficulties* Routledge and Kegan Paul (As accessible approach to language processing and includes a very interesting chapter on comprehension difficulties)

Snowling, M (1987) *Dyslexia: A Cognitive Developmental Perspective* Basil Blackwell (Interesting research into the phonological aspects of dyslexia by an important researcher in this area)

Springer, S and Deutsch, G (1989) *Left Brain, Right Brain* Freeman and Co. (Fascinating and accessible account of research into brain functioning)

Thomson, M (1984) *Developmental Dyslexia* Edward Arnold (Very comprehensive overview of theory, research and teaching)

First Person Accounts

Hampshire, Susan (1981) *Susan's Story* Sidwick, Jackson (Engrossing account of the actress's experience of dyslexia and how it affects her life)

Hampshire, Susan (1990) *Every Letter Counts* Bantam (Interviews with a wide range of adults in various occupations - a useful resource for students)

Simpson, Eileen (1981) *Reversals* Gollancz (A highly recommended description of the experience of undiagnosed dyslexia and of the long struggle towards success)

Teaching and Learning

Baddeley, A (1982) *Your Memory: A User's Guide* Penguin (Pelican). (Interesting resource for the role of memory in learning)

Baddeley, A (1987) *Working Memory* Clarendon (as above)

Buzan, T (1989) *Use Your Head* BBC Books (Offers creative strategies to improve learning and memory)

Buzan, T (1993) *The Mind Map Book: Radiant Thinking* BBC Books (Illustrations and exercises for developing mind mapping)

Chinn, S, J and Ashcroft J R (1993) *Mathematics for Dyslexics: A Teaching Handbook* Whurr Publishers. (Aimed at children but emphasising learning styles in maths and suggests useful strategies for dyslexic learners)

Goodwin, V and Thomson, B (1995) *Adult Students and Dyslexia: A Resource Book for Adult Students and Staff*, (with accompanying audio cassette) Open University (Includes guidance on applications and screening and useful sections on study skills and information technology)

Klein, C and Millar R (199) *Unscrambling Spelling* Hodder and Stoughton (a diagnostic approach to teaching spelling, with many practical activities and photocopiable resource sheets, for use with individuals and in the classroom)

Klein, C (1991) *Setting up a Learning Programme for Dyslexic Adults* Language and Literacy Unit (A practical guide to setting up an individualised spelling and learning programme)

Recommended reading and resources

Klein, C (1992) *Diagnosing Dyslexia* Basic Skills Agency (An approach to diagnostic assessment which can be used as the basis of devising an individualised learning programme)

Reid, G (1994) *Specific Learning Difficulties (Dyslexia): A Handbook for Study and Practice* Moray House Publications, Edinburgh (Primarily a course handbook for teachers of children, it offers a very useful, comprehensive and clear coverage of theory and practice - it is especially valuable for its emphasis on learning styles and its very thorough section on sources and resources)

Rose, C and Goll, L (1992) *Accelerate Your Learning* Accelerated Learning Systems Ltd, 50 Aylesbury Road, Aston Clinton, Aylesbury Bucks HP22 5AH (A very rich resource aimed at transforming students' confidence and results by giving them techniques to learn that match the way they learn best - includes handbooks, video and audio cassettes)

Shaughnessy, M (1977) *Errors and Expectations* Open University Press (not specifically about dyslexia but extremely interesting and useful approach to developing writing skills, such as the use of kernel sentences)

Williams, L V (1986) *Teaching for the Two-sided Mind: A Guide to Right Brain/Left Brain Education* Simon & Schuster Inc (A very stimulating introduction to using 'right brain' strategies to improve learning, with interesting and creative examples)

Other Resources

FEALDS (Further Education and Learning Difficulties Support) National Directory 1995 London Language and Literacy Unit (Gives contact names, addresses and telephone numbers of tutors in Further and Higher Education who are trained to diagnose and support dyslexic students)

Crisfield, J and Smythe, I, eds (1994)*The Dyslexia Handbook* British Dyslexia Association, Reading (A useful general resource)

Matty, J (1995) *Dyslexia: Signposts to Success - a guide for dyslexic adults* British Dyslexia Association, Reading (very useful and practical 'how to' guide to gaining access to assessment, education, employment, training and qualifications)

Videos

Dyslexia: Symptoms (Adult dyslexic students describing their personal experience of how dyslexia affects them in areas such as reading, spelling, memory, direction. Very illuminating and useful) Obtainable from Alpha Training, Chorlton Park Centre, Mauldeth Road West, Manchester M21 25L

The Channel Four "Dyslexia" Video (Features both children and adults of different ages with dyslexia. Shows the suffering and frustration and also the relief and increase in self esteem gained from diagnosis and specialist help) Obtainable from Richard Nathanson, Hopeline Videos, PO 515, London SW15 6LQ